THE THEORY OF VALUE BEFORE ADAM SMITH

THE
THEORY OF VALUE
BEFORE
ADAM SMITH

BY

Hannah R. Sewall

[1901]

THE ADAM SMITH LIBRARY

Reprints of Economic Classics
AUGUSTUS M. KELLEY PUBLISHERS
New York 1968

First Edition 1901

(New York: The Macmillan Company
for The American Economic Association, 1901)

Reprinted 1968 by
AUGUSTUS M. KELLEY · PUBLISHERS
New York   New York   10010

LIBRARY OF CONGRESS CATALOGUE CARD NUMBER

65-26382

PRINTED IN THE UNITED STATES OF AMERICA
by SENTRY PRESS, NEW YORK, N. Y. 10019

CONTENTS.

CHAPTER I.

VALUE BEFORE THE SIXTEENTH CENTURY. JUST PRICE.

CHAPTER II.

VALUE IN THE SIXTEENTH AND SEVENTEENTH CENTURIES. NATURAL VALUE AND EXCHANGE VALUE.

CHAPTER III.

VALUE AND ECONOMIC SCIENCE BEFORE 1776.

CHAPTER I.

The Greeks, in common with most ancient peoples, had no conception of " rational laws governing the phenomena of the distribution of wealth."[1] They studied human conduct to discover a man's duty, or to ascertain what kind of actions constituted noble lives, rather than to know the ultimate relations of all actions. Their object was practical rather than theoretical, and questions of economic relations were closely connected in their minds with questions of right and wrong, with problems of justice.

In consequence of this attitude the somewhat naïve conception of value (ἀξία),[2] or the worth of a thing, as a quality belonging to the thing itself, was not questioned. It was commonly held that the price ought to correspond to this quality, but that it often did not. Plato reflects this thought in the statement that, " when a man undertakes a work, the law gives him the same advice which was given to the seller, that he should not attempt to raise the price, but simply ask the value ; this the law enjoins also on the contractor ; for the craftsman assuredly knows the value of his work."[3] Even Aristotle, who was more scientific than Plato, held this same objective conception, but he recognized more clearly the influence of demand upon value. Aristotle's

[1] Cossa, Introd., 127.

[2] 'Aξία also meant weight, and as money was first passed by weight, ἀξία evidently signified the weight in money ; but it also meant weight in the sense of importance, worth. See Liddell & Scott, *sub verbo*.

[3] Laws, book xi, ch. 921 ; Jowett, vol. 5., p 308.

explanation of value is not only interesting in itself but of great importance because of its influence upon later thought. He discusses the subject almost exclusively in connection with exchange. Exchange, he explains, is due to the needs of men, and arises from the circumstance "that some have too little, and others too much."[1] In order to be exchanged, things must be made equal to one another, and the resulting equation is an expression of value. But value has its basis in utility. "Of everything which we possess," he says, "there are two uses; both belong to the thing as such, but not in the same manner, for one is the proper, the other the improper or secondary use of it. For example, a shoe is used for wear, and is used for exchange; both are uses of the shoe."[2] If, in this passage, Aristotle does not make a clear distinction between value in use and value in exchange, he gives a basis for such distinction. But it is significant that he deems use in exchange to be a subordinate use. "He who gives a shoe in exchange for money or food to him who wants one, does indeed use the shoe as a shoe, but this is not its proper or primary purpose, for a shoe is not made to be an object of barter."[3] It is only because of its primary use that a shoe can be used in this secondary manner.

In the Ethics, Aristotle implies that value is expressed by the proportion in which things exchange for each other. Here he develops his idea of value as a part of the general subject of justice. He has come to that form of justice which he calls corrective justice, which is justice in private transactions whether voluntary or involuntary.[4] Voluntary transactions are such as " sell-

[1] Politics, book i, ch. 9; Jowett, p. 15.
[2] *Ibid.*
[3] *Ibid.*
[4] Ethics, book v, ch. 7; Welldon, p. 145.

ing, buying, lending at interest, giving security, lending without interest, depositing money, hiring."[1] In voluntary exchange a person makes a profit if he gets more than belongs to him. "But when people get as the result of exchange exactly what they had at the beginning, neither more nor less, they are said to have what belongs to them, and to be neither losers nor gainers. That which is just, then, in corrective justice is a mean between profit and loss. . . . It implies that the parties to a transaction have the same amount after it as before."[2]

But how is determined the proportion in which things are to be exchanged? Aristotle thinks that the problem would be easily solved if the labors that produced the things were equal, but, he says, " there is no reason why the work of one should not be superior to that of the other."[3] "For association is formed, not by two doctors, but by a doctor and a husbandman, and generally by people who are different, and not equal, and who need to be equalized."[4] The result of the equalizing will be a proportion in which the amounts of the goods to be exchanged will stand in inverse ratio to the persons who produced them, *i.e.,* " As a husbandman is to a cobbler, so is the cobbler's ware to the husbandman's."[5] In this illustration Aristotle thinks of the persons themselves where we should think of their services as productive agents.[6] But in order to determine the figures

---

[1] Ethics, book v., ch. 7, Welldon, p. 142.
[2] *Ibid.,* book v, ch. 8 ; Welldon, p. 149.
[3] *Ibid.,* p. 151.
[4] *Ibid.,* p. 153.
[5] *Ibid.*
[6] David Parke Ritchie in Palgrave's Dictionary, article "Aristotle," remarks that " We may perhaps make this idea intelligible to ourselves by thinking of the amounts to be given in exchange as in the *inverse ratio* to the value of an hour's labour of each producer."

of such a proportion, there arises the necessity of a "single universal standard of measurement." "This standard is in truth the demand for mutual services, which holds society together; for if people had no wants, . . . either there would be no exchange, or it would not be the same as now."[1] Demand finds a sort of recognized representative in money, which, therefore, "is like a measure that equates things, by making them commensurable."[2] Thus the demand which society has for mutual services is in Aristotle's view the force which determines the values of things and services. The money price is the expression of this value.

This explanation has been commented upon as merely an attempt to bring the familiar phenomena of exchanges into accord with the central thought of Aristotle's ethical philosophy,[3] that virtuous actions follow a mean between two extremes. Justice, *i.e.*, corrective justice, is a mean between profit and loss. That all exchanges were not just exchanges, that all prices did not represent that value which fulfilled the conditions of corrective justice, he was well aware. Money-making by means of exchange, especially by retail trade, he regarded with great disfavor. He especially condemned usury, the breeding of money from money.[4]

The Romans had no theory of value beyond a general conception of a degree of esteem (*estimatio*), or of an equivalence between two things (*pretium*), expressed by the amount of the price (also *pretium*). They recognized that value bore some relation to desire. Cicero, speaking of the great price of bronze statues, said :

---

[1] Ethics, book v, ch. 8 ; Welldon, p. 153.
[2] *Ibid.*, Welldon, p. 154.
[3] Bonar, Philosophy and political economy, p. 40.
[4] Politics, book i, chs. 9-10 ; Jowett, pp. 17-19.

"The only limit to the valuation of such things is the desire which anyone has for them, for it is difficult to set bounds to the price unless you first set bounds to the wish."[1]   But in the main they held that the value of goods commonly exchanged did not depend upon desire but upon what they could sell for, *i.e.* the price ; thus Seneca says: "the price of anything is a temporary accident; however much you may praise your wares, they are worth only as much as they will sell for."[2]   Yet he had just said "that some things are of greater value than the price which we pay for them."   He does not explain the difference between these two aspects of value.

The conception of the relation between price and value was vague and undefined.   Writers upon the law describe price as meaning money accepted in payment for a thing bought, the emphasis being upon money as one of the articles exchanged rather than upon the amount of money accepted.   Thus the jurist Paulus in describing the origin of sales said :   "In early times there was no money, and no distinction in language between 'wares' and 'price', but after the invention of money the word 'wares' is no longer used of both the articles exchanged, but one of them is called the 'price' — so the wares and the price are different things."[3]   Some, on the basis of passages in Homer, thought that if a good was given in payment for a thing bought,[4] the good might be considered as the price.   But Paulus thought that such a transaction was not a sale, but a case of barter, in which there is no 'price'.   The use of money as the price would in time lead to the association

[1] In Verrem, book iv, ch. 7.
[2] De beneficiis, book iv, ch. 25.
[3] Dig., book xviii, tit. i, § 1.
[4] Institutes of Justinian, book iii, tit. xxiii, § 2.

of the concept price with the quantity accepted in an exchange. Furthermore the money being in fact the quantitative expression of the exchange value of the thing bought, there can be little doubt but that the Romans, like most people of to-day, did not distinguish between the value which appears in an exchange, and price, but used the concepts interchangeably. Indeed the two ideas were, as already indicated, expressed by the same term, *pretium*. *Pretium*, however, does not appear to have been an exact equivalent of the modern expression, value-in-exchange; it did not have the same technical signification. It may be said that the Romans apprehended, without comprehending, value-in-exchange. They were not writing treatises upon economic conceptions, but were merely expressing certain relations which occurred in practical life. They did not attempt to discover how prices are determined. In an award of damages it was necessary to have some guide to a fair price. But Paulus writing on this subject was satisfied with maintaining that the price is a common function. He quoted Pedius who said that " the prices of things are to be determined neither with reference to affection nor to their utility to single individuals, but prices have a common validity, (*communiter fungi*)"[3]. Prices were in fact determined by the unrestrained agreement of contracting parties; how they happened to have a "common validity" no Roman undertook to explain.

The Romans were not dominated, as were the Greeks, by ethical conceptions. They did not, like Aristotle, seek to know what prices would accord with the principles of justice, nor like the canonists of later times urge that in every transaction a just price should be

---

[3] Ad legem aquillam, Dig. book ix, tit. ii, § 33.

realized.   A rescript of Diocletian permitted a seller to
recover if the thing were sold for less than half its true
price (*verum pretium*) or value.[1] This was thought by
the Christian Fathers to constitute a limitation upon
the freedom of contract, and is held by a modern
authority[2] to indicate some intention to regulate price
according to ethical conceptions.   But it seems to have
been intended to apply only in special cases.   The law
permitted almost absolute freedom of contract.   It even
went so far as to allow that, as was said by Paulus, " In
buying and selling a man has a natural right to purchase for a small price that which is really more valuable, and to sell at a high price that which is less valuable, and each may seek to overreach the other."[3]   In
this quotation and also in the language of the rescript
there is indicated a conception of a definite " value ", a
characteristic of the particular thing, of which the price
may not be an equivalent.   It may be said that the
Romans apprehended value in two aspects, viz., personal
esteem and the esteem of the buying and selling public,
that the latter was commonly regarded as expressed by
the price, but that there was no essential relation between price and value in the first aspect.

In Greece and Rome economic activities were subordinate to political and esthetic interests, and the
study of economic problems therefore was subordinate
to the solution of the more important problems of ethics
and jurisprudence.   There was no investigation of
economic phenomena for their own sake.   Yet both of
these societies had reached a comparatively advanced
stage of industrial development.   Money economy had

[1] Ashley, vol. 1, p. 208, n. 19.
[2] Endemann, vol. 2, p. 30.
[3] Quoted by Ashley, vol. 1, p. 132 ; p. 208, n. 18.

long been established; there was borrowing and lending of money; production had become capitalistic; and commerce, both foreign and domestic, was active and enterprising. With the barbarian invasions all this was changed. Enterprise ceased and the commercial life of the ancient world was supplanted by a more primitive economy which was destined to prevail throughout Europe for many centuries.

The economy of the barbarians was a natural economy, "a kind of economy," says Prof. Ashley, "in which land was given for service, service given for land, goods exchanged for goods without the intervention of a currency at all."[1] But the economy of the barbarians was characterized not only by an absence of money, but also by an absence of bargaining. Their society was a plexus of personal relationships acquired by birth. Each man was rewarded for his services according to the social status into which he had been born; if a serf he was entitled only to a serf's pay, if a lord he was rewarded as a lord. The conception of value implied by this system is often regarded as a simple labor theory. But it must be remembered that the worth of any good or service was not thought to be determined according to the time or ability of the person making the good or performing the service, but according to his rank in society and the scale of living necessary to maintain that rank. That is, the value of the goods or services depended upon the social rank of the laborer,[2] not on their want satisfying power to the user, which was not thought of except in the broadest and vaguest way.

Society for many centuries after the barbarian inva-

---

[1] Economic history, vol. I, p. 43.

[2] Cf. Aristotle : "As a husbandman is to a cobbler, so is the cobbler's ware to the husbandman's." See ante, p. 3.

sions was composed of communities which, for the
most part, were economically self-sufficient and socially
independent of each other.   Contact with southern
civilization, however, created a taste for articles of
luxury which travelling merchants brought to the
more powerful over-lords, and there was some trading
in the necessaries which could not well be produced on the manor.   In a few towns of considerable
size a trade in food stuffs and manufactured articles
sprang up and was carried on by persons to whom special
privileges had been granted, but who continued to culti-
vate the soil.   In time there also appeared in the towns
handicraftsmen, who lived solely by practicing their
arts and crafts.

About the year 1000 a money economy began, here
and there, to supplant the natural economy.   During the
three following centuries it gradually spread throughout all Europe.   The customary services and dues in
kind in the village communities were commuted by the
over-lords into money payments.   The use of a medium
of exchange which made it possible to produce for a
market, lead to a diversification of employments and
the development of classes devoted exclusively to some
one vocation.

When a natural economy is supplanted by a money
economy, and producers become specialists, the satisfaction of wants comes to depend, in the first instance,
upon purchase rather than upon production.   That
is, the individual who wants anything, goes out and
buys it, instead of sitting down and making it, as under
a natural economy he would commonly have been
obliged to do.   Thus the importance of buying and
selling in the daily lives of the people becomes im-
mensely increased.   It is well known that the ideas

of people are often far behind what their circumstances would lead one to expect. Although the change to a money economy was virtually completed during the middle ages, yet the labor theory of value which is characteristic of a natural economy remained and influenced profoundly most of the thought upon the subject during that period.

After the development of handicrafts the consumer supplied his need of manufactured articles by orders upon the craftsman's labor. The latter had no capital beyond his tools and shop. The consumer supplied the materials, paying only for the labor. This system prevailed everywhere for the first few centuries and in remote countries throughout the middle ages, so that the greater part of the wants of a community were satisfied by the labor performed in that community. Despite the gradually increasing use of a medium of exchange, society was still far from attaining the stage of a money economy such as we know to-day.

A circumstance having greater power to modify the conception of value, appeared in the development of a class of men who bought goods in order to sell them again, the professional trader and the foreign merchant. In foreign trade especially, the distance between the producer and the consumer was so much increased that the service rendered was taken to be that of bringing the goods to the market,[1] rather than that of manufacturing them. The original producer was so far removed from observation, that no estimation of value according to his social position could be made.

The commutation of services for money payments, the growth of handicrafts, the increase of commerce, all represent an industrial revival which began in the

[1] Endemann, vol. 2., p. 43.

11th century. The Christian theologians, who did the thinking for the middle ages, had their attention drawn to economic matters. The ecclesiastical jurists especially, in building up a body of law that should be to the church what the civil law was to the state, found the problem of value forcing itself upon their attention. In dealing with economic subjects they were not actuated by a desire to build up a science; their object was rather to establish rules for the guidance of human conduct. They were not seeking to explain phenomena, but to apply certain principles to existing social conditions, in order that human conduct might follow the course which seemed to them to be laid out for it by divine command.[1]

To the Christian teachers the increase of buying and selling seemed fraught with great spiritual danger. They had been accustomed to regard the amassing of wealth as sin, and had favored an economy based upon the common ownership of property. They were favorable to agriculture, they tolerated manufacture, but they condemned trading, for the latter made no new thing, but encouraged the pursuit of gain for its own sake.[2] Yet the great thinker, Saint Augustine, had seen that wealth could not be wholly condemned, and had argued that it was permissible for the laity to be rich provided they used their possessions for the good of mankind, and did not seek excessive wealth for its own sake. It was impossible also to deny the advantage of commerce,

[1] "It [canonist doctrine] differed from modern economics in being an 'art' rather than a 'science,' . . . . all art indeed in this sense, rests on science, but the science on which the canonist doctrine rested was theology." Ashley, Economic history, vol. 2, p. 379.

[2] While the schoolmen praised agriculture, they said of manufacture, "Deo non displicit," but of trade, "Deo placere non potest." Quoted by Roscher, Geschichte, p. 7.

and as it grew with the opening up of new trade
routes and opportunities, the conservative position became more and more untenable.　In view of the rapid
industrial development wise churchmen recognized that
the church, if she was to maintain her position as the
pilot of the people, must steer with the current and not
against it, that she should point out and define the conditions under which trading might be permissible, and
not merely condemn it.　The problem was two-fold :
first, to reconcile a progressive money economy which
they could not but see was advantageous to mankind,
with Christian ethics which dwelt upon the spiritual
danger of wealth and of gain for its own sake ; and second, to protect the economically weak against the economically strong.

In the thirteenth century translations of the works
of Aristotle began to be numerous, and the teachings of
this great philosopher began at once to influence the
thought of the schoolmen.　His writings were found to
lend a powerful support to their doctrines, and were constantly referred to as authority.　Like him the Christian
theologians believed that a just exchange was one in
which equal value should be exchanged for equal value.
They sometimes speak of value as a degree of esteem,
sometimes as the attribute of a thing.　But in general they
conceive of everything that is exchanged as having
some one true value, which is not known through
individual esteem, but rather through the general estimation of the community.　This depends, in turn, upon
the labor that has been exerted upon the thing, estimated in accordance with the social rank of the laborer,
and the standard of living that belongs with that rank.
This idea, as we have seen, was the outcome of the still
prevailing natural economy, and it was supported by

the scriptural text, "the laborer is worthy of his hire."
Albertus Magnus went one step farther, he saw that
there was a social necessity that the laborer should be
paid his price, since otherwise the product of his toil
would not continue to be supplied to the community.[1]

The justification of an exchange was to be found in
the presence of a just price, which was that price which
expressed the true value.[2]   The Christian theologians
thought that the prices, especially of articles of every day
consumption, should be fixed by the civil authority ; but
as economic relations became complicated it became
more and more difficult to recognize the just price ;
how this could be done by those whose duty it was to
fix the price, was the problem they undertook to solve.

The most important treatise upon all the economic
problems that interested Christian philosophers, was
that contained in the Summa Theologica of Thomas
Aquinas.[3]   St. Thomas entered upon these subjects,
however, not for the guidance of legislators, but because
he was writing an encyclopedia of all theology destined
particularly for the instruction of priests.   His doctrines formed the basis of thought after his time and
were much quoted and relied upon as authority.

Like Aristotle, he includes what he has to say on
value and price in a treatment of the general subject
of Justice.   When he comes to justice in relation to
trade, he sets himself the following questions to
answer : 1. Whether it is allowable to sell a thing for
more than it is worth.   2. Whether a sale is made un-

---

[1] He said : "Si enim lectorum factor pro lecto non tantum et tale
accipiat, quantum et quale posuit in expensis, lectum de coetero non
faciet et sit destructur ars quae lectorum factrix est." Quoted by
Graziani, Teoria del valore, p. 14.

[2] Endemann, vol. 2, pp. 14, 36.

[3] Written between 1266 and 1274.

lawful by a defect in the article sold.   3. Is the seller
bound to reveal a fault in an article?   4. Is it right in
trade to buy cheap and sell dear?[1]

The first question he answers in the negative: 1st.
On the ground that the thing proposed is against the
Golden Rule.   "But no one wishes a thing to be sold
to him for a higher price than it is worth.   Therefore
no one ought to sell a thing to another for a higher
price than it is worth."   2nd. That it is unjust in
itself.   "We can speak of buying and selling in two
ways," he says, "on the one hand in itself; and on
this score, buying and selling seems to have been
entered into for the common advantage of both parties,
since, indeed, one lacks what the other has, and the re-
verse, as is shown by the Philosopher in 1 Polit., Chap.
5 and 6.   But what is entered into for common advantage ought not to be more burdensome to one party
concerned than to the other.   Therefore an agreement
ought to be arranged between them in accordance with
an equality of advantage.   But the value of the property which is useful to man is measured by a price
given; for this money was invented, as is said in V
Ethic.   And, therefore, if either the price exceeds the
value, or conversely the value exceeds the price of the
thing, the balance of justice is destroyed.   And, therefore, to sell a thing dearer or to buy a thing cheaper
than it is worth, is, in itself, unjust."   The other case
of buying and selling is where the need of the purchaser
is so much greater than that of the seller, that he will
suffer positive injury if he goes without the article he
desires to buy.   "In this case the just price will not
only take in consideration the thing which is sold, but

[1] Summa Theologica, Secunda Secundae, Quaestio lxxvii.   Thomae
Equinatis Opera Omnia.   Antwerp, 1612, vol. 19, p. 179.

the loss which the seller incurs from the sale.   And so
it would be possible lawfully to sell a thing for more
than it is worth in itself, although it would not be sold
for more than it is worth to the one possessing it." [1]
This case is really an exception to the general principle
already established, viz., that it is unjust to sell a thing
for more than it is worth.

Apart from emphasizing the moral nature of the conception of just price, these quotations from Thomas
Aquinas show first, that he assumes that everything has
a true value, a "what it is worth," which is something
belonging to the object itself, and is not necessarily expressed by what it sells for, *i.e.*, its price; and second,
that this worth or true value is not necessarily the
estimate which either the seller or the buyer, prompted
by their needs or desires, may put upon it.

Aquinas and the canonists attached the same meaning
to the word price that the term had in the civil law;
that is, they meant by it the money given by a purchaser for goods obtained from a seller.   They saw no
necessary correspondence between value and price.[2] But
if the quantity of money given equalled in value the
goods purchased, then the price was a just one and
might be said to express the value.   This lack of essential correspondence between value and price was due to
the character of the conception of value, not to the definition of price, which however serves to cast additional
light upon it.   The canonists did not mean by value

---

[1] Quaestio lxxvii, art. 1, Opera, vol. 19, pp. 179, 180.

[2] This is shown by the quotation just given.   Aquinas' own words
are: "Sed nullus vult sibi rem vendi carius quam valeat. . . . . .
Quantitas autem rei, quae in usum nominis venit, mensuratur secundum pretium datum, ad quod est inventum numisma, ut dicitur in V
Ethic. Et ideo si pretium vel excedat quantitatem valoris rei, vele
converso, res excedat pretium, tolletur justitiae aequalitas." Quaestio
lxxvii, art. 1, Opera, vol. 19, p. 179.

what a thing would bring in the market, that is, exchange value, but some essential characteristic of the thing in itself. We have now to see what considerations established the worth of a thing in itself or its "true" value, as they conceived of it.

We shall be in a better position to answer this question when we have seen what Thomas Aquinas thought ought to be considered in estimating a just price. In his treatment of the second question, whether a sale is made unlawful by a defect in the article sold, to which the general answer is in the affirmative, he offers as a negative argument this : that many dealers are without the knowledge necessary to tell the true qualities of things. To which he replies : "It must be said, as Augustine said in XI De Civit. Dei (Cap. 16), that 'the price of salable things is not reckoned in accordance with the rank of nature, since sometimes one horse is sold for more than one slave ; but is reckoned in accordance with the extent to which the things are useful to man. Therefore it is not necessary that the seller or buyer should know the hidden qualities of the thing sold, but only those through which it is rendered useful to man, for instance that the horse is strong and runs well. These qualities the buyer and seller can easily recognize." [1]

To the third question, whether a seller is obliged to reveal a fault in an article for sale, Aquinas answers that a seller may sometimes keep silent in regard to a secret fault provided the purchaser does not thereby suffer an injury. He then brings up this objection : that it is not necessary ever to reveal a fault, because sometimes the price is reduced when there is no fault, as when there is an increase in the supply of a commodity.

[1] Quaestio lxxvii, art. ii. Opera, vol. 19, p. 180.

To this he replies: "a fault in a thing causes it to be at the present time of less value than it appears. But in the case cited, the article is expected to be of less value in the future on account of the arrival of more traders whom the buyers are not looking for. Whence the seller who sells his wares at the price which he finds current does not seem to act contrary to justice, in not making known what is about to happen." "Yet if he made it known" St. Thomas adds, "or deducted from the price, it would be an act of greater virtue, although he would not seem to be bound to do this on the score of justice."[1]

In these passages Aquinas recognized that both the service-giving quality of an article, or its utility,[2] and the quantity offered for sale influence both value and price, and he held that the price determined by these influences was not unjust, provided that in the transaction there was no intention of fraud on either side. He had already described just price as the price which corresponds to what a thing is worth, its true value; in the last quotation he shows that the just price can be known by the price which the seller finds current on the market to which he brings his goods, *i.e.*, by the common estimation of what they are worth. But when other sellers bring more of the same goods and the price falls, that also is a just price, but each good has some one just price which may vary from time to time, according to the circumstances of the market. In another place he says, speaking of the restitution for injury done by a

---

[1] Quaestio lxxvii, art. iii. Opera, vol. 19, pp. 180–181.

[2] But the utility here referred to is usefulness in relation to an objective end. The utility of a thing in relation to individual need he has shown to be often in excess of value, "as happens when some one needs a thing especially, either for avoiding danger or gaining some advantage." Quaestio lxxvii, art. i, Opera vol. 19, p. 180.

wrongful price, that "the just price cannot always be exactly determined, but is rather a matter of estimation ; so that a little added or taken away does not destroy the balance of justice." [1]

A specific statement of the items that ought to be considered in the estimation of the just price of anything is given by Aquinas in the reply to the fourth question. The first three questions had to do with buying and selling where the sellers had themselves produced the goods which they offered for sale. It is significant of the economy of the time that this case is treated of first as the most familiar kind of buying and selling. The case indicated by the fourth question, where the seller buys his wares for the purpose of selling them, had only lately come into prominence. The question whether it is just to buy cheap and sell dear, is not so easy to answer as the others, and requires careful consideration. Aquinas' reply is a qualified affirmative. He says, "To trade for the sake of obtaining the necessaries of life is lawful for all ; but to trade for gain, unless the gain is destined to some honorable end, is in its nature base." The justness of the transaction lies in the motive of the trader. Such honorable ends are served " when one applies the moderate gain which he seeks by trading to the support of his household, or even to succoring the poor ; or even when one gives his attention to trade for the public welfare, that, indeed, his native country may not be without things necessary to life ; and he seeks the gain not as an end, but as the wages of labor." One can lawfully sell higher than he buys, "either because he has improved the article in some respect, or because the price of the article has been changed on account of difference of place or time,

[1] Quaestio lxxvii, art. i.

or on account of the danger to which he exposes himself in transferring the article from place to place, or in causing it to be transferred." [1]

The transaction being just under these circumstances, a price which includes a fair reward for the trader's service would be just. Thus the just price is a price which recompenses labor and risk, and recoups the merchant for any expenses that he has incurred in transporting the good to market. It is a price that covers all the expenses of production, and of bringing the article to market, but it should not be more than enough to cover these expenses, it should not include any elements of pure profit or gain on account of a differential advantage, since the gain which the merchant is allowed to make should be no more than can be properly considered as his wages. This gain ought to be no greater than what would accord with the proper standard of living for his class in society.

The idea which underlies the reasoning of Thomas Aquinas seems to be that while value is the importance attached to things either by individuals separately or by the community as a whole, the latter only is the "true" value that gives the measure of the just price. Thus the way by which the "true" value of goods produced at a distance could be known was by ascertaining the common estimation of the importance of the same goods in the place to which they were brought to be sold. Of goods produced at home the true value was very well known and was represented by a customary price. There was little difficulty in determining the just price so long as the prevailing economy remained close to the so called "natural" type, but when such complicating agencies as money and middlemen began

[1] Quaestio lxxvii, art. iv, passim. Opera, vol. 19, p. 181.

to appear this became difficult, because the true value itself or the community's estimate of many things fluctuated and they ceased to have a customary price.

Moreover, the idea of "true value" was associated with the social estimation of the sacrifice required to produce things, with the labor that had been expended upon them rather than with the satisfaction that would be derived from using them. The real worth of a thing was thus considered to be equal to its necessary cost. Aquinas, however, not failing to recognize that the useful qualities of a good often influence the estimation of its importance and thus help to make the value, accords utility a place among the items to be considered in reckoning price, but the main emphasis in his discussion is upon items of cost. This conception of cost as related to value had been considerably enlarged by the advent of the trader and importer, and the "true value" of a good brought from afar had come to be thought equal to a cost that included the labor of the merchant, his risks, and his expenses, one of which was that of transportation. The ideas of Aquinas regarding place utility were not very clear. Thus bringing goods from afar was not thought to add to their value because a good was more desirable at hand than at a distance, but because a certain expense needed to be recompensed.

The doctrine of just price gained distinctness and definition from the discussion of usury. Following the teaching of scripture the church had always maintained that it was wrong to take payment for the use of money, and had forbidden the clergy to accept such payments. Later, in the 12th century, this prohibition was extended to the laity. Growing industrial activi-

ties and better living had no doubt increased the demand
for loans.

The prohibition was based not primarily upon the
reason given by Aristotle that usury was the breeding
of money from money,[1] but upon the distinction between "consumptibles" and "fungibles." The former
were those goods that are consumed by using them, as
food stuff; the latter those which are not so consumed,
as a piece of land, in which case the use could be separated from the good and treated by itself. Money was
classed with consumptibles; its use was in spending it
and could not be separated from the thing itself, which
was conceived to be consumed when the visible coin
passed from the hand.[2] To lend money, therefore, according to Thomas Aquinas,[3] was tantamount to a sale,
and to sell a thing and then demand payment for the
use of it was unjust, for it was to demand payment for
what did not exist. The fact that a considerable time
might elapse between the conclusion of the so called
sale and the payment for the thing bought by the
return of the money did not justify an addition to the
price, for it was said that time was common property,
and no one had any right to buy or sell it.[4] The prohibition of usury was commonly evaded under the form
of buying and selling, by giving credit to a buyer or
permission to a seller to delay the delivery of goods,

---

[1] Politics, book I, ch. 10; see also Ashley, Econ. hist., vol. I, p.
152, *et seq.*

[2] "Pecunia autem, secundum Philosophum in quinto Ethicor et in
primo Polit. principaliter est inventa ad commutationes faciendas; et
ita proprius, et principalis pecuniae usus est ipsius consumptio, sine
distractio, secundum quod in commutationes expenditur." Thomas
Aquinas, Summa Theol. Secunda Secundae, Quaestio lxxviii, art.
i. Opera, vol. 19, p. 182.

[3] *Ibid,* p. 181.

[4] Ashley, Econ. hist., vol. I, p. 156; Roscher, Geschichte, p. 7.

the consideration being in the first case an addition to the present price, and in the second, a deduction. This practice was declared to be sinful in a decretal of Alexander II, in 1176, and again by Urban III, in 1186.[1] In order to prevent this evasion of the usury prohibition, it became necessary that the conception of the just price and the marks by which it could be known should be clearly defined. The writings of the canonists, from Thomas Aquinas on, show that this necessity was well understood, and that the writers were well aware how easily a design to exact usury could be concealed under the form of a sale.[2]

During the time when the prohibition against the taking of interest was vigorously supported by the church there was virtually no capitalistic production, and but few opportunities for the profitable investment of money. Those who had money which they did not wish to use themselves, lost nothing by permitting it to be used by others who could give good security for its return. Since the original owner lost nothing during this time by not having in his possession that which he would not have used if he had had it, the canonists did not realize that time could have anything to do with value. The true value of a good was its current value in a community, the common estimation in which it was held. It was derived chiefly from a consideration of what the good had cost, of the just and appropriate remuneration for the labor that had been expended upon it, that is from the past of the good, from what had been put into it, rather than from what was expected to be gotten out of it.[3] Hence the value of a good that

---

[1] Endemann, Studien, vol. 2, pp. 4, 5.

[2] *Ibid.*, vol. 2, ch. 5, § 1.

[3] Cunningham, Eng. industry and commerce, vol. 1, p. 461.

was lent, a " consumptible ", or a sum of money, was its
current value in the community,—the value which it
had to the lender, not that which it might have to the
borrower, for on account of his needs it might have
to him a greater value than the current value.   Hence
the conception that to this person a greater sum of
money or a greater quantity of goods to be paid over at
a future time might be of the same value as a smaller
amount at the present time, was entirely foreign to
canonistic thought.   Thus, as they did not realize the
influence of place on value, no more did they realize the
influence of time.   They did not consider that a good
near the consumer in place and time is of greater value
to him than the like good at a distance from him in
both place and time.

The practical result of the doctrine of just price was
the regulation of price by civil authority.   This was
thought to be especially necessary in the case of goods
of common use, while rare articles, as paintings and
statuary, or articles of luxury, were left to find their
prices through free competition or local custom.[1]   The
multitude of laws having for their end not only the
regulation of prices but of the currency, of weights and
measures and the qualities of the wares offered for sale,
in fact, " every sort of economic transaction in which
individual self-interest seemed to lead to injustice," [2]
shows that the doctrines of the ecclesiastical teachers
and legists were very generally accepted throughout
Europe.

After the time of Thomas Aquinas both foreign and
internal commerce developed rapidly.   Western Europe
became studded with local fairs, at which traveling

[1] Graziani, Teoria del valori, p. 77.
[2] Ashley, Econ. hist., vol. i, p. 181.

merchants, following certain great routes of traffic, stopped to sell wares brought, perhaps, from far off India or China, and with the proceeds to buy goods that had been produced in the neighborhood, to carry away in their trains for sale at other fairs.   Great trading centers, such as the Italian cities and Hanse towns increased in number and importance.   In these cities manufactures, depending upon foreign trade for the disposal of their products, were carried on upon an extensive scale. There was everywhere a tendency towards greater division of labor and specialization of employment, accompanied always by a more extensive local traffic. This development reacted upon the theologians and upon their doctrines.   The subjects of value, price, commerce and credit were discussed with increasing fullness ; the earlier doctrines undergoing considerable modification and development.[1]   Some of the more important writers were John Nider of Swabia, St. Anthony of Florence, and St. Bernard of Sienna.

The most important modification of the earlier doctrine showed itself in the tendency to neglect cost as the foundation of true or common value, and to substitute utility. Cost, however, was still reckoned in price. This tendency was due to increasing supplies of goods coming into the local market, which were produced at such a distance that little could be known of the cost of manufacturing them. Therefore the general or social esteem in which they were held was derived chiefly from the serviceable qualities of the goods, and from the desire which people had to possess them. This social esteem or common value, was sufficiently definite to be used in a

---

[1] For some account of the literature of trade and value, see Endemann, Studien, vol. 2, ch. 5, § 1 ; and Stintzing, Geschichte, p. 539. Also Cossa, Introduction, p. 150.

rough way to base the just price upon. But the merchant
who brought in these goods performed a service for the
community for which he should be paid. The social
esteem or common value of the goods should be high
enough to cover this item, or the trade would not be carried on. The common value was held to give, therefore,
a starting point from which to reckon the just price.[1]

As to the formation of value, St. Anthony[2] considered that it was due to the interaction of three elements. First, the general usefulness of a good in satisfying wants; this he considered the cause of value.
Second, its scarcity ; this raises the value. Third, that
quality which renders it more or less pleasing to the
individual. This in special cases can be the cause of
increasing price.

St. Bernard justified trade on the grounds of general
utility, of special utility to the one who bought the
goods, and of particular utility to the merchant on account of his profit. This profit he maintained was just,
as the fruit of his industry, diligence and talent. " Just
price, " he added, " is what conforms to the valuation
of the place, that is, to what the subject of a sale is
commonly thought to be worth at such a time and at
such a place ; "[3] and when one transports goods from
one place to another he can sell them at the price of
the last place. Endemann points out that this circumstance gave the foreign merchant a great advantage
over the local trader and even opened the door to specu-
lative gain.[4] But it was a logical consequence of the
doctrine that the just price should be reckoned from

---

[1] Endemann, vol. 2, p. 40, *et seq.*

[2] Summa Theologica. See Graziani, Teoria del valore, pp. 18, 19.

[3] S. Bernadino, Istruzioni morali succitali, pp. 107–110.   See Graziani, pp. 19, 20.

[4] Studien, vol. 2, p. 45.

the common value of the place.   St. Bernard also
named the items that ought to be considered by public
authorities in establishing legal prices.   These were
the natural utility of the good, its abundance or scarcity,
the peril, fatigue and industry of those who procured it
and preserved it and otherwise inconvenienced themselves for the advantage of others.   The retribution for
personal services, he considered, should depend upon
the character of the services, whether skilled or un-
skilled, and their dignity.[1]

Nider,[2] whose treatment of the subject is more extensive and systematic than that of his predecessors,[3]
named five points which it is necessary to consider in
judging whether a price be just.   First, whether the
good "is better for human use", that is, from the point
of view of the buyer.   Second, whether it "is becoming
better in the estimation of man", that is, whether a
general demand for it is growing.   "This might happen
if it remained unaltered in quality or even became
worse; especially if a new and unusual need for it developed, as a thing availing against infection since it
might then be very properly sold dearer than at other
times."   In this connection Nider lays down the general principle that goods can be sold only as they are
esteemed; but then, he says, every seller of a particular
thing is a suspected judge, so one must heed the estimation of the generality.   Third, protection against
loss, but in this case a seller can not raise the price
above the judgment of the buyers.   Fourth, the service
of the merchants, which Nider takes pains to justify,
considering it as deserving of reward as that of the ar-

[1] Graziani, p. 19.
[2] He wrote Tractatus de contractibus mercatorum, 1435.
[3] Stintzing, p. 543.

tificer, for " the labor of the one may be just as pleasing
and desirable to men as of the other." Fifth, whether
the just price is known through law, custom, or
through commerce. This is probably a reference to
the three kinds of prices all of which existed in Nider's
time, (1435), namely legal price, customary price, and
competitive price. Nider finally said that, because of
these circumstances, it may not be possible to discover
the exact just price, and one will have to be satisfied
with a probability.[1]

As a natural consequence of the growth of commerce which increased the number of articles actually sold at competitive prices, it became less and
less easy to determine an exact just price ; hence
the canonists were compelled to allow some latitude.
St. Anthony thought the price actually paid just, provided there was no excess against conscience. And
Nider thought it was not necessary "to reach an indivisible point of equivalance." The just price might
be so made up " that a small addition or diminution is
not seen to bear against justice."

Thus the main modifications in the mediaeval doctrine of value and price after the time of Aquinas were,
placing greater emphasis upon utility as the cause of
value, and allowing greater latitude for variation in the
just price. Just price was that price which paid
for the labor, the expense, and risk of the merchant. It
could conform to the value of the good both when derived from the intrinsic qualities which make it serviceable, and from the qualities which make it capable of
satisfying some peculiar fancy or desire. There was a

---

[1] For a sketch of the contents of Nider's work see Endemann,
Studien, vol. 2, pp. 7, 8. See also Zuckerkandl, Theorie des Preises,
pp. 36, 37.

fundamental difference between the conceptions of usefulness and desirableness. The former was objective
and social, the latter subjective and individual. The
failure to reconcile these two conceptions, to compre-
hend subjective utility, was not confined to mediaeval
thinkers, and is, no doubt, responsible for the comparative lateness of a satisfactory explanation of value on
the basis of utility.

This sketch of the conception of value in the middle
ages is not complete without some account of the ideas
of the canonists upon the value of money. They recognized under the general conception of exchange or
barter three different transactions, namely, the exchange of a thing with a thing, barter proper; of money
with money, which was *cambium* or exchange in the
narrow sense; and finally, of a thing with money, which
was a sale.[1] Each was regarded as a complete transaction in itself, and hence the intermediary character of
the last two was completely overlooked. Money
was thought to have two functions; it served as a
measure of value, by exchanging in turn for different
wares; and it became a means of gain to its owner, by
serving as an object of an exchange. In the latter case
it occupied the position of the ware, while the money
given for it was the price, called the *valuta*. The canonists, with their view of an objective true value which
could not be known from subjective valuations, held fast
to the opinion that when money was used as a medium
of exchange the value was placed upon it by authority,
that is, by the power which had the right of coinage. The
value of money was, therefore, the nominal value of the
coins.[2]

[1] Endemann, Studien, vol. 2, p. 11.
[2] *Ibid*, vol. 2, pp. 172–199.

The determination of the just price of money in the second use was a matter of great importance, first on account of the great number of civil powers having the right of coinage, and the many different kinds of coins ; and second, on account of the ease with which the lending of money for usury might be concealed under the form of an exchange.

The exchange of money for money was regarded as exactly parallel to the exchange of goods for money, hence the permissibility of a particular case would be decided by the same rules.   Technically the exchange was the barter of the money given by the money changer, *i.e.*, the seller, for the *valuta*, the money given by the buyer.   If the *valuta* was greater than the sum exchanged for it, the excess was characteristically justified by the canonists on the ground of the labor or trouble to which the exchanger had been put to effect the exchange.   His occupation was admitted to be serviceable and necessary to society, and therefore, deserved a suitable compensation.[1]   No charges above this just reward ought to be permitted.   There ought to be no giving or accepting payment for credit, since this would be usury.   The trade of the money changer, like all other trade, they thought, ought to be regulated by the civil authority.

An exchange between moneys of different lands was known as a real exchange.   The exchange between moneys of different kinds in different places was considered as an extension of the real exchange, and the exchanger was entitled to a recompense for the labor of transportation as well as for the labor of exchange. This latter exchange was usually effected by means of a bill of exchange on a distant place payable in the de-

---

[1] Endemann, Studien, vol. I, pp. 211, 212.

sired kind of coin. There was no actual carrying of money, but later canonists considered that there was an imaginary transportation for which the exchanger was entitled to recompense.[1]

The actual rate of exchange did not follow the nominal value of the coin, but the value of the metal. This fact led the canonists gradually, as they came to lay greater stress upon objective utility as a basis of the value of goods, to the view that in the exchange of moneys the value of the money was founded upon its intrinsic goodness, that is upon the quantity and fineness the metal in the coin.

Roscher points out that the Christian theologians did not reach the conception of universal value, or value in the abstract; that they did not perceive that although material was used up and tools worn away that value remained, reappearing in the product; that, therefore, they failed to realize the nature of capital.[2] However this may be, they certainly "did not group together certain forms of wealth, employed for a particular purpose, under a general conception or designation."[3] Prof. Ashley maintains that "the absence of any such conscious grasp of the conception of capital as we now possess may, indeed, be traced back to the absence of a still more fundamental idea in modern economics, the idea of exchange-value (or of 'value' itself in the limited sense attached to the term by English writers). The thinkers of the middle ages only very gradually worked their way from the conception of a number of particular things possessing a value-in-use-to-particular-persons, to the conception of general exchanging and purchasing

[1] Endemann, Studien, vol. 1, pp. 110, 111.
[2] Geschichte, p. 7.
[3] Ashley, Economic history, vol. 2, pp. 394, 395.

power." " The conception of exchange-value" the same writer continues " could only come into existence as goods and services began to be increasingly exchanged one for another, instead of being made for the maker's own use; as they began to be increasingly reckoned in the same measure of value, and thus comparison became easy; that is, when a ' money economy' supplanted a ' natural economy.' The growth of the conception must have followed, and could not precede the growth of the fact." " It may be allowed " he adds, " that the thought of the canonists in this respect lagged behind the progress of circumstances." They were held back by their ethical and religious motives and prejudices. Hence, other circumstances besides favorable economic conditions were necessary for a more complete analysis of value, and for the special development of the conception of exchange value.

CHAPTER II.

VALUE IN THE SIXTEENTH AND SEVENTEENTH CENTURIES.—NATURAL VALUE AND EXCHANGE VALUE.

In the sixteenth and seventeenth centuries economic questions were no longer the concern exclusively of moralists and writers upon jurisprudence. The general substitution of an economy based upon buying and selling for that based upon personal service, and especially the growth of a national economy, gave new importance to industrial problems and brought into prominence a new class of writers known as empiricists. Whether the empiricists dealt with particular economic problems, such as are concerned with money, prices, or foreign exchanges, or developed empirical systems and discussed politics, the aim of their writings, one and all, was to advance the material prosperity of the nation to which they belonged. Thus their purpose, like that of the canonists, was practical, but their enquiries were concerned with the adaptation of means to ends, with the discovery and application of remedies for existing difficulties, while the mediæval moralists had been concerned only with the distinction between what is proper and permissible, and what is vicious. In the history of value, this difference is of great importance. To the canonists no other than an ethical view of the subject was possible. The purpose of their lay successors called not for a justification, but an explanation, of value. The problem is no longer what value should be, but what it is.

It is true that the ecclesiastical writers and moral philosophers who treated of value during the period now

to be considered, still held to the Aristotelian classification, making economics a part of politics and politics a
part of ethics.   In the systems of ethical jurisprudence,
based upon the conception of natural law, it was necessary to discuss value and price before passing judgment
upon those contracts which involve exchanges of things.
The spirit and point of view of the churchmen and
philosophers that treated value in this period were much
the same as those of their predecessors, the canonists, but
were somewhat altered by changed conditions and the
views of the empiricists.   The recognition of value as
involving an economic as well as a moral problem,
marks the most distinct advance.

The gradual turning of the scholastic philosophers,
during the later middle ages, from the task of present-
ing doctrine to that of finding proofs, led to a revival
of the study of nature, which was at length followed not
so much for the sake of these proofs as for its own sake.[1]
With this revival a renewed emphasis was placed upon
natural law, which was considered to be a veritable
branch of jurisprudence and the foundation of positive
law.   It was the law implanted in man by God and
making itself felt through his conscience and reason.
Grotius derived it from the "appetite" of man for
society, by reason of which he "has a faculty of know-
ing and acting according to general principles," and
also from God since the social nature of man was of
divine origin.[2] Thus natural law having its origin in
human nature, a previously established condition, it
could not be altered by the author of that condition any
more than he could prevent two and two from being
four.   Natural law was conceived to find its sanction

[1] Erdmann, History of philosophy, § 213.
[2] Grotius, De jure belli et pacis, prol. § 7 *et seq.*

in itself, since any act was obligatory or unlawful in itself, according as it was in agreement or disagreement with the rational or social nature of man, and hence commanded or forbidden by God, the author of nature.[1] The conception of natural law, therefore, placed before the minds of men a set of positive rules having divine sanction and made known to them in this character by the "dictate of right reason."[2] The general belief in the reality of such law was of immense usefulness in bringing about that criticism and reconstruction of systems of jurisprudence which constitutes the special contribution of these centuries.

The influence of this conception upon the particular subject that we have before us was of great importance. It justified what circumstances had increasingly brought about, namely, the determination of actual prices by competition, not by authority. Natural law did not deny but affirmed the old canonist principle that the validity of a contract depended upon the principle of equality of advantage. But it suggested the inference that if two persons, similarly situated, made an agreement and both were satisfied, in the very nature of the case neither would suffer any disadvantage, and if the agreement involved a price, that price would not be unjust.[3]

After touching briefly upon the views of some of the ecclesiastical moralists which may be considered fairly representative of the thought of the class upon value, we will consider more at length the views of

---

[1] Grotius, De jure belli et pacis, book i, ch. 1, § 10.

[2] *Ibid.*

[3] The earlier canonists probably would not have denied this proposition. They differed from these later writers, however, in believing that equality of advantage depended upon objective rather than upon subjective conditions.

Grotius and Puffendorf, representing the writers upon jurisprudence, and finally we will consider as representative of empirical thought the views of the Italians, Davanzati and Montanari, and of the Englishmen, Nicholas Barbon and John Locke.

The tendency to justify competitive prices is seen in the works of many Italian churchmen of the 16th century. Thus Sabba da Castiglioni upheld liberty of contract, although he believed that just and reasonable prices for public property should be determined by authority.[1] Also Buoninsegni, a friar who began life as a trader,[2] affirmed the existence of laws of trade independent of legislative will. He wrote that if buyers and sellers, without fraud or violence, contract freely, it lies in the very nature of the case that the price which is accepted by both will be just; a thing is worth as much as it commonly sells for, that is as much as the buyer and seller agree upon in the absence of fraud or blundering. The increase or decrease of any price is the result of mutual consideration at the time, of the abundance or scarcity of the subject of the transaction, and of the great or small number of sellers and buyers. "Therefore, when there is a plenty of buyers, price increases, and it decreases when there is a multitude of sellers." He also considered as legitimate a sale at a price somewhat higher when payment is to follow sometime after the delivery of the merchandise, because if the buyer accepts the agreement he cannot consider himself damaged.[3]

Somewhat similar language was used by Sig. Scaccia, an ecclesiastical jurist who, early in the seventeenth

[1] Graziani, Teoria del valore, p. 24.
[2] Cossa, Introduction, etc., p. 154.
[3] Tommaso Buoninsegni, Della traffichi guisti ed ordinarii, 1591. See Graziani, pp. 24, 25.

century, published an extensive work upon commerce and exchange [1] which reflected the most advanced views of his day; indeed, so liberal was his thought that for a time his work rested under the ban of the church, but was finally declared to contain nothing contrary to canon law.[2] He maintained that the just price was not an indivisible point but had an upper and lower limit; that there was a highest, a medium, and a lowest just price. That if prices were fixed by a superior power the just price would be " that price in which is included the estimation of the intrinsic good of the thing itself, of its abundance, of the expense and labor which is required to transport it from one place to another, also of the care and expense which must be employed to preserve it, and of the risk which the seller assumes in acquiring it and in transporting it." But since in the absence of a legal price the just and natural price could be known only by certain objective features of the transaction, Scaccia offered the following as criteria by which it could be recognized. " Just price is that price which is commonly sought in respect to any object by one who is not in want, and it is equal to what can be obtained from one not in want, who is intelligent and knows the condition of the object and has full age and sound mind." [3]   That is to say, that whenever opposite parties, acting under conditions which insure equality of advantage, agree upon a price, it is in the nature of things a just price.

The Reformation, so far as economic thought is concerned, brought no immediate advancement. It was a revolt against the corruption of the Roman curia, not

[1] Tractatus de commerciis et cambiis, Rome, 1618; Cossa, 151.
[2] Endemann, Studien, vol. 1, p. 54.
[3] Quoted by Endemann, Studien, vol. 2, p. 40. See also Zucker-kandl, Zur Theorie des Preises, p. 68.

against the philosophical and ethical teaching of ecclesiastical writers. In economic opinion indeed, it was marked by a return to the doctrines of the earlier canonists. Luther thought that wealth was dangerous to the spiritual health, but that everyone should be rewarded according to his work or his service. He praised agriculture and handiwork and admitted the necessity of trade, but he thought it difficult for the trader to be without sin, and the most zealous ecclesiastical moralist of the 13th century scarcely rivalled him in invectives against usury.[1]

The religious wars of the 16th century called out Grotius' great work upon the relations of nations in war and peace,[2] in which he maintained that human conduct in war as well as in peace should be subject to the law of nature. In his chapter upon contracts he is led to consider value. He brings up the subject as a phenomenon of nature, so that we obtain his conception of it from direct statement, and not by inference from the discussion of a problem involving the idea of value, as in the case of Aquinas and the canonists. He considers need the most natural measure of value, "as Aristotle rightly shows," and probably the only measure among barbarians, but among civilized peoples the "will of men which is the master of things desires many things more than are necessary," hence desire is also a measure. But "as it comes to pass" that "the most necessary things are of small value for their abundance," it happens "that a thing is supposed to be of such value as is given or offered for it commonly," to which there is necessarily a certain latitude. Thus value which is the estimation in which a thing is held, varies according

---

[1] Wiskemann, p. 47 *et seq.*
[2] De jure belli et pacis.

to the common price. " For that common price," Grotius continues, " account is commonly taken of the labor
and expense of the sellers, and it undergoes sudden
changes according to the excess or defect of buyers,
money and wares." [1] This statement though brief is
significant. Grotius is not thinking of the just price, but
of the current price which would be the natural result
of a comparatively free competition of buyers and sellers,
and he makes no attempt, as did Scaccia, to identify the
one with the other.

Grotius was followed by Puffendorf [2] who devoted a
chapter of his work, " Of the Law of Nature and of
Nations," to a much more extensive analysis of value.
He derives the law of nature from the social nature of
man, and hence its most fundamental principle is the
obligation to " promote and preserve a peaceful sociableness, whence all actions which necessarily conduce to
this mutual sociableness, are commanded by the law
of nature, and all those on the contrary are forbidden,
which tend to its disturbance, or dissolution." [3] Armed
with this criterion he seeks to discover what is in accordance with and what is against the law of nature in
all departments of human conduct, including, of
course, that in relation to property. [4]

As things that are subject to ownership must often
be exchanged in order that they may be properly dis-
tributed among men, " it becomes necessary for men to
agree upon some common measure, by which things of
a different nature may be compared together, and made
equal to one another." This common measure he con-

[1] De jure belli et pacis, book ii, ch. 12, § 14.
[2] Grotius published in 1623, Puffendorf in 1672.
[3] Of the law of nature and nations, book ii, ch. 3, p. 115, (Oxford, 1710).
[4] *Ibid.*, book v, ch. 1.

ceives to be the capacity of things for " having a value put upon them." " But since things receive a value, not only from their natural substance, but also in respect to some moral consideration, it follows that besides the natural, there must also be a moral quantity." " This," he says, " we call price, which is the moral quantity or value of things or actions, by which they are usually compared together in order to traffick." Thus Puffendorf uses the word value in a broader sense than price, while the latter has the usual meaning of value in economics.   His conception is that value is attributed to things and actions by society irrespective of exchange.   When things are brought together to be exchanged their values are compared.   The fundamental cause of value he states as follows : " The foundation of the price or value of any action or thing is, fitness to procure either mediately or immediately, the necessaries, or conveniences, or pleasures of human life."   The explanation which follows shows that his thought was chiefly fixed upon utility.   He says " hence in common discourse we call those things that are useless, things of no value ;—thus the cock in the fable set no value upon the jewel, because of no use to him."

In entering upon the discussion of what causes price to rise and fall, Puffendorf notes that the price of a thing does not always correspond to the " eminency " of its use.   " Nay, we generally find the most necessary things are cheapest, because by the peculiar providence of God nature affords a greater increase of them." Accordingly, " that which chiefly raises the price is scarcity."   The reason for this is because " the ambition of mortals esteems those things most which few men have in common with them ; and, on the other side, thinks meanly of those which are seen in the hands of

everyone. But generally we set a great value upon
nothing but what raises us in some measure above the
rank and condition of others; and for this reason
honours, particularly, are more valuable for being
scarce." Puffendorf thinks all this proceeds, indeed,
"from the corruption and pravity of human nature.
For my goods are never the worse because others possess the like; nor better because others want them.
He therefore that prides himself in seeing others want
the good things that he is master of, seems indeed to
take pleasure in other men's misfortunes." Furthermore, "it ought to be ranked among the senseless
opinions of the common people, to value things either
for their being new, or scarce, or hard to be gotten, or
brought from far, unless their goodness also and their
usefulness recommend them." In the case of things in
daily use, especially "such as relate to provision, ap-
parel and arms," they rise in price when they become
necessary as well as scarce. " The prices of artificial
things, besides the scarcity of them, are much raised by
the neatness of the art; the reputation of the artificer
adds credit to some, and others are more valuable for
the character of their former possessor." "In short,
the difficulty, the elegancy, the usefulness, necessity of
the work, the scarcity of workmen, their being masters
in the art, their not being under a necessity of working,
all contribute to the raising of the price."

Thus far Puffendorf has been dealing with the general causes which, if left to themselves, always affect
prices, and he has shown that these causes act indirectly
by first affecting the dispositions and inclinations of
men. In a state of nature, therefore, the price of anything would be whatever the contracting parties should
agree upon. He next treats of the effect of advanced

civilization on prices. In a regular government prices are determined either by "an order from the magistrate, or some laws, or else by the common judgment and estimate of men, together with the consent of the parties." The former he calls "legal price", the latter "natural price"; the former is fixed "in a point" but the latter "admits of some latitude" "by reason of which it is generally divided into three degrees, the lowest or favourable, the middle or reasonable, the highest or rigorous; within which degrees a thing may be bought or sold dearer or cheaper." And "that may be said to be the just price, which is generally agreed upon by those who sufficiently understand the market and the commodities." "In regulating this natural price" he says, "regard is to be had to the labor and expense of the merchant in importing and taking care of his goods." Risk also should be paid for, and lastly the seller should be recompensed for selling at a time less favorable to him, or for loss on account of slow payment; "for a day is part of the price, which is more if paid down upon the nail, than if paid some time after." Regard must also be had for the circumstances of the market, for "what sudden and frequent alterations the market admits of by reason of the plenty or scarcity of buyers, money or commodities, is well known."[1] In this we recognize much that is already familiar in canonistic discussions.

Puffendorf evidently conceives value to be the esteem in which a good is commonly held by the community. The term rendered by his translator, "natural price" is, in the original, *pretium commune*, which clearly has this meaning. It is distinguished from the more general term, *pretium vulgare*, which is

---

[1] Of the law of nature and nations, book v, ch. i, passin.

the esteem a man in the state of nature feels.[1] He also had a definite conception of value as actual capacity or power in exchange, but he applied it to money alone. In the first part of his discussion he distinguished between two kinds of prices; *pretium vulgare* and *pretium eminens*, by the first meaning the value of goods for human use, by the second, the value that is set upon money. His own words are: " Price may be divided into *proper (vulgare)* and *eminent*, the *first* is *placed* in things and sections, so far as they are capable of procuring either the necessaries, or conveniences, or pleasures of life : The *other* is placed in money, which is supposed to contain *virtually* the prices of all things else, and to be the common measure and standard of them."[2] This distinction must not be confounded with that between real and nominal price, for the term eminent price is applied only to money, and means the capacity of money for exchanging for things, or in other words the exchange value of money. Because of a need of a medium of exchange, " most civilized nations by agreement thought fit to set a certain eminent price upon some particular thing, as a measure and standard for the price of every thing else; by the help of which one might procure any salable commodity, and commerce might be carried on more conveniently." [3]

Puffendorf condemns any arbitrary tampering with the value of money by magistrates, since the convenience of the public depends upon this being kept as nearly constant as possible.   He sees in land the nearest possible approach to an unchangeable standard of value ; it is capable of being compared with respect to quantity with other things; " for from it, mediately or immediately,

---

[1] Of the law of nature and nations, p. 368 n.
[2] *Ibid.*, book v, ch. 1, § 3, pp. 368–9.
[3] *Ibid.*, § 12.

proceeds most things that human life subsists upon. And the product of it being one year with another pretty equal, it may be presumed to have its natural value fixed and certain, to which the prices of other things, at least, of such as have not received their value from the luxury or folly of man, are referred to as to a standard." Since land is in private hands, the value of money "must needs rise, or fall according as it is scarce or plentiful, in proportion to land."[1] But Puffendorf also points out another cause for a change in the value of money with the change in its quantity, and this is the natural price of the metal of which it is made. "For since metal as to its natural price may be, and often is, brought into commerce as well as other commodities, its value must rise and fall according to the scarcity or plenty of it. And the eminent price of money must necessarily follow the natural price of the metals; for it is unreasonable that a quantity of silver, considered as a commodity, should bear a very different price from what it does when considered as money."[2] This opinion was an advanced one, for most people at that time thought that the value[3] of money was purely conventional, and bore no relation to the value of the metal, and that it became less or greater only as its quantity became greater or less in proportion to other things.

Puffendorf also shows advance, as did Grotius, in treating of value as a phenomenon of nature. His discussion of the foundation of value and of what causes it to rise and fall are, from the point of view in which they are presented, contributions to economic theory. But in regard to the determination of value in civilized

---

[1] Puffendorf, Of the law of nature and nations, book v, ch. 1, § 15.
[2] *Ibid.*, book v, ch. 1, § 16.
[3] The exchange value, not the "intrinsic" value. See *post.* p. 51.

society, the ethical and juridical conceptions of the middle ages still dominate his thought. His conception of exchange value and the application of it to money alone, is the special characteristic of the value theory of the period to which he belonged, a period preëminently of transition, during which the function of money as an intermediary in exchange was but vaguely conceived.

Turning now to the other class of writers upon economic subjects during this period, the empiricists, who were called into prominence by the growth of an economic system based upon exchange, and by a national economy, it will be necessary to examine more closely these changes in order to appreciate their influence upon thought.

As intercourse between peoples increases, industrial relations becomes complex. The economic system is more and more based on exchange. It has been said that "the long death struggle of the middle ages" began "with the close of the crusades."[1] They were indeed the beginning of a more active intercourse, not only between east and west, but among western peoples themselves, an intercourse which touched all sides of life. The struggle of princes for supremacy, and of church and papacy to maintain their authority, the rise of new communities, the development of commerce, and the general intellectual growth which make the history of the next three centuries, were all different phases and forms of increasing intercourse which received a second grand impulse from the discovery of America.

The most important as regards our present study were the accompanying changes in the modes by which wealth was produced and wants satisfied. The economic

[1] Erdmann, History of philosophy, vol. 1, p. 546.

system may be regarded as composed of two subordinate systems, that of production and that of regulation. The effect of increasing intercourse upon production was to make it capitalistic. There is probably no time in the history of human industry when labor is not aided by the use of tools or instruments of some sort, at least, no time after the primeval savage found that he could hit harder with a stone than with his naked hand. But capital in a historical sense and capitalistic production are products of an advanced civilization. They come gradually into prominence as the wealth of a people increases faster than its population, and as its tastes become more varied and refined, requiring more elaborate methods to produce what will satisfy them. The progress of capital and capitalistic production became rapid during the 16th and 17th centuries.

Probably no one thing did more to hasten it than the discovery of the silver mines of the new world. The influx of new money rapidly increasing the means by which wealth is transferred made it more available for use in productive enterprises.[1] The immediate effect of the great rise of prices was to put higher profits in the hands of those who would be most likely to use any surplus as capital. Not that the total wealth was necessarily increased but its distribution was altered in such a way that a more rapid formation of capital was inevitable.

During the period before us the regulative part of the economic system had been undergoing changes no less significant than those taking place in the productive part. As production theretofore had been prevailingly local, all that was needed being for the most part produced on the spot and for the particular con-

[1] Cunningham, English industry and commerce, vol. 2, p. 77.

sumer, so economic control had been the function of local organizations and had centered in small communities having a certain degree of political autonomy, such as the village community and the corporate town. Later, as some of these communities expanded into city republics or were included in territorial principalities, economic control was seen spread out over larger areas and concerned with a greater variety of interests; it was coming to be conterminous with the nation itself. The history of the middle ages is a history of the progress·of nation states to a position of power and self-conscious unity; it was inevitable that when the proper time came economic interests should also be made to contribute to national greatness and superiority. This Schmoller has ably shown to be the real significance of mercantilism. "In its innermost kernel," he says, "it is nothing but state-making,—not state-making in a narrow sense, but state-making and national economy-making at the same time. The essence of the system lies not in some doctrine of money, or of the balance of trade; not in tariff barriers, protective duties, or navigation laws; but in something far greater:—namely, in the total transformation of society and its organization, as well as of the state and its institutions, in the replacing of a local and territorial economic policy by that of the national state."[1]

The expansion of the system of regulation to the territorial limits of the state was made possible by the expansion of productive methods, and in turn it aided powerfully to develop the economic system as a whole. With the substitution of national for local markets, industries on a large scale became possible. Intercommunication and exchange

[1] The mercantile system, pp. 50–51.

was facilitated not only by the removal of the petty restrictions by which local bodies had protected themselves from the interference and competition of the outside world, but also by the establishment of common currencies, common weights and measures, postal and banking systems. Interdependence and community of interests was established over a vast territory, including within itself a much greater variety of individual demands than was possible in a single local centre.

The great meaning of these economic changes is that the system of economy based upon exchange became established as we know it to-day. Although commerce and interlocal trade became of considerable importance long before the close of the middle ages, yet it is probable that a large portion of the people, especially in the lower ranks of life, even so late as the middle of the 15th century, still depended upon the direct personal services of their neighbors for the satisfaction of most of their everyday wants.[1] Buying could be done only on stated market days or at the local fairs which occurred only at wide intervals; the store and storekeeper so familiar to us hardly became a common feature in economic life until after the 15th century. The industry of the retail dealer and middleman, requiring that capital should be plentiful and markets extensive, was especially the product of later centuries.

The increase of money and its comparative cheapness after the mines of Potosi began to be worked by the Spaniards, had of course an important influence in promoting exchange in every day life. This end was also

[1] See the account by Prof. Ashley of the development of a class of middlemen in the woollen industry, Economic history, § 44, vol. 2, p. 209 *et seq*.

furthered by the use of bills of exchange and banking facilities, which attained a high degree of perfection during this period. On account of the immense confusion growing out of the great variety of coins, money dealers had adopted a system of money of account which had for its unit an ideal coin of a specified weight in gold, with which they settled balances among themselves.[1] But the national policy which aimed to give to the people a currency which should be uniform throughout the nation, did more than anything else to facilitate exchanges in the humbler walks of life.

An extensive and complicated economic system based upon exchange would inevitably give rise to a conception of value as exchange power. It would seem that any person in possession of goods had only to offer them for sale to possess a certain number or quantity of any other goods that he might want, and the power of obtaining other goods which the possession of certain goods bestowed on him would be associated in his mind with the goods themselves as their exchange value. Money was the first good to acquire exchange value and it was a long time before the conception of mutual exchangeability was attached to other goods in the same degree. The mediaeval manner of regarding the exchanges of goods with money, and of money with money, as final transactions, continued to wield a subtle influence upon the judgment, and the full force of the meaning and place of money as a medium of exchange was scarcely comprehended until well into the 18th century.

The position of money as having purchasing power *par excellence*, as is well known, was the source of some of the most important features in mercantile policy.

[1] Handbuch des Handelsrechts, p. 312, article "Goldschmidt". Endemann, Studien, vol. 1, p. 182.

While wealth was not considered as has often been erroneously asserted, to consist only of money or the precious metals,[1] yet the quantity of the precious metals in circulation in a country was held to be the index of its wealth and its prosperity. "Gold and silver" said Locke, "though they serve for a few, yet they command all the conveniences of life, and therefore, in a plenty of them consists riches."[2] Hence, it was held that a country in order to grow richer should take care to prevent the exportation of its money or to draw in as much as possible from foreign countries. The former policy, which was at first the more important, afterwards partially gave way to the theory that if money were exported in commerce it would bring in more money provided a balance favorable to the nation exporting it were secured on each series of transactions. Thus said Thomas Mun: "The ordinary means therefore to increase our wealth and treasure is by foreign trade, wherein we must ever observe this rule; to sell more to strangers yearly than we consume of theirs in value. For in this case it cometh to pass in the stock of a kingdom, as in the estate of a private man."[3] As a private individual to grow rich must be careful to spend less each year than his income, so, it was held, a nation must buy less in value from other nations than it sells to them.

The service of mercantilism to economic theory is not so much in the doctrines it actually developed or that may be drawn from its practice, as in the industrial experiences it made possible. The experiences growing out of the commercial policy which are chiefly identified with mercantilism and which were of undoubted in-

[1] Ingram, History of political economy, p. 37.
[2] Considerations of the lowering of interest, Works vol. ii, p. 9.
[3] England's Treasure by forraign trade, pp. 7, 8.

fluence upon ideas, were still of less importance than
those growing out of the extension of industrial peace
and comparative freedom to larger areas and between
greater numbers of interests ; and out of larger conceptions of economic unity and social prosperity. It was
the observation of the manifold industries of his native
Kirkaldy, their mutual relations among themselves and
the mutual relations of town and country that taught
Adam Smith the elements of political economy.

Yet we must guard against picturing to ourselves any
great advance in the direction of local freedom of trade
under the mercantile system. The mediaeval notion
that if in trading one party gained more than his legitimate wages he did so at the expense of the other, still
held sway over ordinary minds and influenced the policy
of legislators. On the other hand people were beginning
to see that the guidance of self interest was necessary to
enterprise and to the prosperity of the nation. Thus to
guard the people against the merchants' greed for profit
many old restrictions were retained, and to encourage
the development of industry in those directions which
seemed to make most for national prosperity, inducements
were offered that had indirectly the effect of restrictions
upon the less esteemed industries. In order that nations
might have goods to export for the goods and money of
foreign nations, manufactures were encouraged at the
expense of agriculture, and manufactures for the foreign
market at the expense of those for the home market.

Although the subject of value received on the whole
scant treatment by the empirical writers of this period,
and this is especially marked when we consider the vast
number of monographs, essays and tracts that make up
its economic literature, there was a conception of value
that was tacitly accepted and often referred to in more

or less distinct terms in writings on such other subjects as money, coinage and trade.

In the common thought of the people this conception scarcely differed from that of the canonists, whose practical judgments they accepted. It was objective, *i.e.*, value was thought of as if it were a property of commodities. There were two kinds of value, intrinsic value, which corresponded to true value as conceived by the canonists; and value, without qualifying adjective, which meant price, the two terms being used interchangeably. This distinction appears in a statement of Montchretien de Vatteville, who said, in reply to a statement made in regard to the high prices which had followed the influx of gold and silver from America, " that the essential value of merchandise is unchangeable, not the accidental price, which depends on many things for more or less." [1] He maintained that there was no proportion between the prices of things and the quantity of money. The intrinsic value of money was understood to be equal to that of the metal it contained, and the debasement of the coinage was depreciated; but many of the same writers also held that the exchange value of money was determined by the government stamp, and went so far as to concede the propriety on the part of a prince of lowering the intrinsic value if he should be in unusual need.

It was upon the conception of exchange value or price as something within the control of arbitrary power, as well as upon the superior importance attached to money, that the doctrines of the mercantile school rested. But deeper reflection, a stronger mental grasp of the subject of money in all its relations, and of commerce, not unfrequently led to an analysis of exchange value as having

[1] Traicte de l'oeconomie politique, p. 257.

a natural cause, and to a construction in broad outlines of a value theory. In this work the Italian writers are especially important ; they saw that value derives its existence not from the goods themselves but from their relation to human need. Thus Giovanni Peri, a merchant, and a contemporary of Scaccia, wished that the price paid for the subject of a purchase might be equal to the value of it, meaning by value not a physical quality of the thing but the esteem in which it is held because of its capacity to serve human needs.[1] Peri does not seem to have a conception of exchange value, since he distinguishes between the price of the thing and its value. But later we find this conception appearing with considerable definiteness, almost replacing the value-in-use of the middle ages, which, however, remains, in popular conception as intrinsic value. But the more acute thinkers were well aware that the conception of an unchangeable intrinsic value was false. They also disregarded cost as an element in determining the magnitude of exchange value, accounting for it rather by the relations of utility and need. The reason for this no doubt lies in the fact that they regarded their subject from the standpoint of exchange and not, as did the canonists from the standpoint of production, but the canonists had no conception of exchange value, they were concerned only with concrete prices.

One of the earliest Italian writers of importance was Bernardo Davanzati, who like Peri, was a merchant. His little book published in 1588, was entitled Lessons upon Money ;[2] and his object in writing it was to show the harm that comes from debasing the coinage. In this book[3] he asserts that the price or exchange value

---

[1] Graziani, Teoria del valore, p. 28.

[2] Lezione della moneta. Scrittori classici, tomo ii, Milano, 1804.

[3] *Ibid.*, pp. 30–35.

of goods bears no proportional relation to their natural qualities. Money also he claims does not derive its purchasing power from the natural qualities of the metals of which it is composed, but from the agreement of people to employ them as instruments of exchange. He illustrates this principle as follows,—"An egg," he says, "the price of which may be half a grain of gold, sufficed to keep the count Ugolino alive in the Tower of Famine for eleven days, whilst all the gold of this world would not have been sufficient."[1] "What is of more importance to life than wheat? Yet ten thousand grains of wheat sell for a grain of gold. How happens it, then, that things by nature so valuable are worth so little gold? And according to what principle does it happen that one thing is worth so much more than another?"[2] This he explains substantially as follows : —that all the things in the world which men desire with which to satisfy their wants in order that they may be happy, are in the aggregate equal in value to all the money, *i. e.*, gold, silver and copper, which is in circulation, because men by common consent have agreed to exchange the metals and the commodities with each other. Thence it follows that the amount of money which any given thing is worth bears a proportion to the whole amount equal to the proportion which the happiness it is capable of procuring bears to the whole happiness of a people. Passing over the value of goods in money, this explanation evidently contains the idea that the values of goods relatively to one another depend upon the happiness they are capable of procuring, or, as we would say, upon their subjective utilities. Davanzati does not dwell upon this con-

[1] Lezione della moneta, p. 31.
[2] *Ibid.*, p. 32.

ception ; it is quite evident that he was far from comprehending its importance.

He passes on to show that an exact mathematical expression of the relative values of goods is an impossibility; since to arrive at it would require the consideration of a variety of circumstances quite beyond the power of man to include in one calculation. But he shows that they are roughly expressed in the prices at which things are actually bought and sold, and therefore the merchant is the best judge of them. In the illustrations which follow, Davanzati brings forward two kinds of circumstances which affect values, the quantity of goods in relation to the need for them, and special desirable qualities. " A disgusting thing is a rat," he says, " but in the siege of Casalino one of them was sold for 200 florins on account of the great scarcity, and it was not dear because he who sold it died of hunger and he who bought it escaped." " Vases, painting, statues, pictures and other merchandise are bought at excessive prices by men of pride because they find so great a part of their beauty in the fact that they are worth so much gold. Similarly the men of Peru exchanged at first for pieces of gold a mirror, a needle and a bell, because these new and marvelous things made more display, and they found more happiness in them than in the gold which abounded." [1] Thus Davanzati in a rough way presents the conception that utility is a function of quantity and desirability. It is significant of the real importance of Davanzati's conception, that the utility upon which value depends in his theory is not objective but subjective, it is the capacity for producing happiness from the side of the nature of man and not from the side of

[1] Lezione della moneta, pp. 34, 35.

the natural qualities of the object, that he has in view.
Thus the difference between his position and that of
the Austrian economists is even less than would at first
seem to be the case. Yet there is no comparison between the two, or rather they bear the relation to each
other that a vague opinion bears to an extended scientific
analysis.[1]

Geminiano Montanari, writing on money nearly a
century after Davanzati,[2] gave a similar explanation of value, but it was worked out in much greater
detail. His book[3] was probably written with much
the same purpose, for he praises the invention of money
which has made the whole world as one city, since any
man who has money can buy anything he needs in any
part of the globe. Money, he claims, measures· the
quantities of all things, even our desires and passions.
It is a measure of desire because the amount that we
spend for a thing corresponds to our appetite for it.
But, he explains, money can only be regarded as the
appropriate measure of things that are finite, it cannot
measure the insatiable desires of the avaricious. As
money measures desires so desires become the measure
of money and of value. For the support of this last
proposition Montanari appeals to the authority of
Aristotle, who maintained that the universal measure
of value is the wants of people which find a common
representative in money.[4] Therefore the desires of
men measure the values of things to which money
ought to conform ; from which it follows that desires
or wants measure the value of money no less than of

[1] On Davanzati, see also Graziani, Teoria del valore, pp. 30, 31, and
Zuckerkandl, Theorie des Preises, pp. 46, 47.
[2] About 1680.
[3] Della moneta. Scrittori classici, tomo iii, Milano, 1804.
[4] Ante p. 4.

things, and *vice versa,* money measures wants and desires no less than it measures the values of things.[1]
Montinari evidently means that desires, money, and
things, bear such a relation to each other that whatever
decides the position of one determines that of the others.
Whence he is led to support the proposition of Davanzati, that the mass of goods in exchange varies in value
with the actual amount of money in circulation, so that
if there were no change in the quantity of goods, a
change in the amount of money would be followed by a
change in prices.[2] This somewhat crude statement of
a quantity theory of money, taking no account of
rapidity of circulation, was no doubt suggested by the
phenomenon of rising prices that followed the influx of
American treasure.

Having established this theory to his satisfaction
Montanari next takes up the question of the relative
values of goods.[3] Given the quantity of money, what
decides the values of particular commodities? The
general answer is their scarcity or abundance. But
how does the scarcity or abundance of commodities de-
cide their value? Montanari thinks that the explanation is plain and notorious, yet nevertheless it will help
the understanding to give it some attention. "I understand a thing to abound," he says, "not when as a
matter of fact there is a great quantity of it absolutely,
but when there is a great abundance of it in relation to
the need, esteem and desire which men have for it."[4]
In this sense scarcity renders any commodity precious
and abundance renders it cheap. Thus "given the

---

[1] Della moneta, ch. 2, p. 40 *et seq.*
[2] *Ibid.,* 45.
[3] *Ibid.,* ch. 3.
[4] *Ibid.,* p. 59.

amount of money in circulation, to change the esteem
that men have for things changes price, it becoming
higher if desire increases, and lower if the goods fall
into disfavor." [1] These quotations show that Montanari understood in a general way that exchange value
is determined by personal valuations, but he makes no
attempt to explain the details of the process. That a
personal valuation is dependent upon the subjective
utility is also implied in his explanation. He takes
some pains to establish the proposition that wants must
be interpreted as meaning not only the needs of men,
but also their desires, and that therefore the same law
controls the values of the necessities and the luxuries
of life. He maintains that this was Aristotle's meaning. [2] However this may be, Montanari has here taken
a position which is essential to a scientific explanation
of value from want-satisfying-power or utility. That
position was not reached in the middle ages because of
the inability of mediæval thought to rise above the
particular. Want then meant only lack of a necessity ;
lack of a luxury was another thing and quite different.

The dependence of esteem upon fashion and other
external circumstances is set out at considerable length
by Montanari. Of these the most influential are the
desires of princes. "There is no power," he says "to
change suddenly the prices of things in the world so
great as the esteem in which princes hold them. Cara-
calla caused yellow amber to bear a great price throughout the Roman Empire by ordering it imported for his
ornaments because it was the color of his mistress's
hair. ' Whatever princes do seems to instruct.' " [3]

[1] Della moneta, p. 61.
[2] *Ibid.*, pp. 43–45.
[3] *Ibid.*, p. 61. See also on Montanari, Graziani, pp. 31–35 and
uckerkandle, pp. 48, 49.

The doctrine that value is not an intrinsic quality of things but depends upon their relation to variable human wants was also set forth by an English pamphleteer, Nicholas Barbon,[1] in a tract entitled A Discourse of Trade, published in 1690. His position in regard to the nature of wants and utility was essentially the same as that of Montanari.

He considered the use of things which " are to supply the wants and necessities of man" to be the source of value. He classified " wares useful to supply wants" under the two general heads, of those " useful to supply the wants of the body," and those useful to supply the " wants of the mind." Of the former " which are useful to supply the three general necessities of man, food, clothes, and lodging," if " strictly examined" only food is absolutely necessary. " Wares that have their value from supplying the wants of the mind, are all such things that can satisfy desire ; desire implies want : it is the appetite of the soul, and is as natural to the soul, as hunger to the body." " The wants of the mind are infinite, man naturally aspires, and as his mind is elevated, his senses grow more refined, and more capable of delight; his desires are enlarged, and his wants increase with his wishes, which is for everything that is rare, can gratify his senses, adorn his body, and promote the ease, pleasure, and pomp of life." " Things rare and difficult to be obtained" have value because they " are general badges of honour: from this use, pearls, diamonds, and precious stones have their value."

What Barbon has described in these few sentences is merely the esteem which is felt for the things by the individual or by the community. He next proceeds to show that there is a close relation between this esteem and exchange value or price. "The price of wares is the present value; and ariseth by computing the occasions or use for them, with the quantity to serve that occasion; for the value of things depending on the use of them, the *over-plus* of those wares, which are more than can be used, become worth nothing; so that plenty, in respect of the occasion, makes things cheap; and scarcity dear." As personal value is variable because of external circumstances and of the circumstances of the mind, so also is exchange value and for the same reasons. "There is no fixed price or value of anything, for the wares of trades, the animals, and vegetables of the earth, depend on the influence of heaven, which sometimes causes murrains, dearth, famine, and sometimes years of great plenty; therefore, the value of things must accordingly alter. Besides, the use of most things being to supply the wants of the mind, and not the necessities of the body; and those wants, most of them proceding from imagination, the mind changeth; the things grow out of use, and so lose their value."

As prices cannot be fixed, those asked by persons who have wares to dispose of, represent only a rough estimate of value. "There are two ways by which the value of things are a little guessed at; by the price of the merchant, and the price of the artificer: the price that the merchant sets upon his wares, is by reckoning prime cost, charges and interest. The price of the artificer, is by reckoning the cost of the materials, with the time of working them; the price of time is according to the value of the art, and the skill of the artist. . . . Interest is the rule that the merchant trades by; and time, the artificer, by which they cast up profit, and loss; . . . . but the market is the best judge of value ; for by the concourse of buyers and sellers, the quantity of wares, and the occasion for them are best known. Things are just worth so much, as they can be sold for, according to the old rule, *valet quantum vendi potest.*" [1] Barbon's idea evidently was that market value is determined by the competition of subjective valuations, and that it is the expression, more or less accurate, of the worth of things,—of the esteem in which they are held by society or by the individual.

Barbon had a much clearer idea than his contemporaries of the nature of rent and interest, he also showed the falsity of the prevailing theory of the balance of trade. But he made one great mistake, he contended that the value of coins depended upon the stamp affixed to them by the government. It has been suggested that this error may have been the cause of the oblivion into which his writings fell in spite of their great merits.[2] But his ideas were in advance of the times while others more in accord with the current tendencies of thought were set forth by no less a person than John Locke, who was destined to have a permanent influence upon economics as well as upon other departments of knowledge. Locke's conception of value belongs in quite a different line of development from that represented by Barbon and by Davanzati and Montanari. What he presented was a careful analysis, or theoretical explanation, of the conception of value in the common thought of the people. He was in advance of it, however, in that he showed that exchange value is not accidental but is the natural result of existing conditions. Though there is much to be desired in his analysis, we

---

[1] Discourse of trade, quoted by Cunningham, English industry and commerce, vol. ii, p. 229. See also article upon Barbon by Steven Bauer, in Palgrave's Dictionary.

[2] McCulloch, Literature of political economy, p. 157.

find in it the conception of value as power in exchange fully developed. Locke approached the subject of value from two points of view, that of the philosopher dealing with first principles, and that of the pamphleteer or empiricist. It is from the latter position in his "Considerations upon the lowering of interest and raising the value of money" that he had most to say on exchange value. Therefore we shall confine ourselves at present to this position, leaving the former to be considered later.

Locke regarded natural law as the way things go on in the absence of restrictive rules, such as men who have agreed to enter into association with one another make for the good of themselves.[1] The tendency of his thought was to regard nature's way as the best; he believed that it would be for the advantage of society to allow such economic phenomena as the rate of interest to determine themselves according to natural law. Since the "natural" rate is that which men agree upon among themselves according to the dictates of their private interests, it is therefore that which will encourage the most profitable use of money. In showing how the natural rate is determined, Locke was led to review the causes of value.

Intrinsic or natural value, he explains, depends upon utility, while marketable value is a relation in exchange. Thus "the intrinsick natural worth of anything, consists in its fitness to supply the necessities, or serve the conveniences of human life; and the more necessary it is to our being, or the more it contributes to our well being, the greater is its worth." But "the marketable value of any assigned quantities of two, or more commodities, are *pro hic et nunc* equal, when

[1] Civ. Gov't. Works (1726), vol. ii, p. 160, *et seq.*

they will exchange one for another." Nor do these
two kinds of value rest in any proportion to each other,
that is, "there is no such intrinsick natural settled
value in any thing, as to make any assigned quantity of
it, constantly worth any assigned quantity of another."
He does not mean to imply, however, that intrinsic
value has no connection whatever with marketable
value, on the contrary it is essential to the existence of
the latter, since the " vent of anything, " that is, its sale,
is shown to depend upon its necessity or usefulness.[1]

Marketable value or exchange value is merely a proportion in which two things which are exchanged stand
to one another. "The change of the marketable value
of any commodity, . . . is not the altering of any intrinsick value or quality in the commodity ; (for musty
and smutty corn will sell dearer at one time than the
clean and sweet at another) but the alteration of some
proportion, which that commodity bears to something
else." [2]

Locke's statement of that upon which the amount of
marketable value depends is rather obscure. He says :
" He, that will justly estimate the value of any thing,
must consider its quantity in proportion to its vent, for
this alone regulates the price." [3] Vent, he explains,
" is nothing else, but the passing of commodities from
one owner to another in exchange." [4] The vent is
regulated by the rapidity with which commodities are
bought up and removed " out of the way and course of
trade." [5] This is shown to be due ultimately to the
consumption. Thus while Locke by vent evidently re-

[1] Considerations, etc., Works, vol. ii, p. 21.
[2] *Ibid.*, p. 22.
[3] *Ibid.*, p. 20.
[4] *Ibid.*, p. 22.
[5] *Idem.*

fers to the demand side in the determination of value, he did not reach an accurate conception of demand, and as also he did not even attempt to develop the supply side his explanation leaves much to be desired. It was not, however, with the value of commodities that he was especially concerned in this essay but with the value of money.

It is not a fault of the mercantile theory that it represented money as important on account of the power to own other forms of wealth, present and future, bestowed by it upon its possessor; but that it stopped there, thus giving the impression that this power dwelt in the money itself, and not in the fact that other forms of wealth existed and were being reproduced as fast as wanted. That this was not really the opinion of mercantilists is proved by the theory not uncommon among them that money obtained its value solely from the agreement of society to use it as a medium of exchange, and that its value would therefore depend upon the proportion between the quantity of money on the one hand and other forms of wealth on the other. This was the opinion, as we have seen, of such men as Davanzati and Montanari, and stands in contrast to that other opinion, also prevalent, that the value of money was whatever the government decreed it should be, by the stamp it put upon its coins. This latter view was held by Barbon who maintained, in answer to Locke, that apart from law, the value of money was like the value of the metals, which varied in different times and places, as the values of other things. Locke on the other hand held the value of money to be a matter of convention. Money serves, he explains, in two ways, the one for reckoning by its stamp and denomination; the other for exchanging valuable things, " by its intrinsick value, which is its quantity." Mankind, he asserts, have put an "imaginary value" upon the precious metals, because by reason of their fitness for this purpose, they " have made them, by general consent, the common pledges, whereby men are assured, in exchange for them, to receive equally valuable things, to those they parted with, for any quantity of these metals. By which means it comes to pass, that the intrinsick value, regarded in these metals, made the common barter, is nothing but the quantity, which men give or receive of them."[1] Locke feels that there must be a difference between the " intrinsick" value of money and of other things because they serve by being sooner or later used up, that is consumed ; while money serves only by being passed from hand to hand as pledges for other goods and is not used up.[2] He fails to see that there is no essential difference between the two utilities, and that, therefore, the value which is attributed on account of utility in the latter case, is no more imaginary than that in the former. By saying that the "intrinsick" value of money is nothing but its quantity, he implies that money really has no intrinsick value but only exchange value. This is as it were " a double value," *i. e.*, it is a value which may be derived from either of two sources. The first is the power of money of affording an income to its owner, and in this he compares money to land, the value of which " consists in this, that by its constant production of salable commodities, it brings in a certain yearly income ;" the second is the power of money of procuring for its owner by exchange the necessaries and conveniences of life. In the latter aspect, money is like

---

[1] Considerations, etc., Works vol. ii, p. 12.
[2] *Ibid.*, p. 17.

any other commodity except that it serves only by exchange and can have only exchange value, the amount
of which, like that of other commodities, is determined by
its quantity in proportion to its vent." [1] The value of
all commodities including money in circulation consists,
according to Locke, in a proportion, whence it follows
that an alteration in the quantity of the money produces
a change of value, but the change of value is in the
money, not in the commodities, therefore, trade remaining the same, the quantity of money in circulation
regulates its value. The serviceableness of money in
trade, its power " to drive the trade" of a country is the
source of its value. This value will increase if the
profit to the borrower increase, which will happen if
the quantity of money decrease in proportion to trade,
or to the vent of all commodities, taken together. Accordingly Locke maintains that when the quantity of
money increases, interest, which is the income afforded
by money, diminishes, because the exchange value of
the money being less, the borrower cannot make so
large a profit with a given amount of money as formerly. [2]
Such reasoning by so astute a philosopher and so careful
an observer shows that in the economic opinion of the
17th century the way money performs its functions was
still far from being understood.

Locke confused money with capital. In this respect,
as indeed in most points of the theory of value he was
behind Barbon, who declared it to be a mistake to consider interest a payment for money, that in reality it is
a payment for stock. It is " the rent of stock " he said,
" and is the same as the rent of land. The first is the

[1] Considerations, etc., Works, vol. ii, p. 17.
[2] *Ibid.*, p. 23.

rent of wrought or artificial stock; the latter of un-
wrought or natural stock." [1]

The confusion between money and capital was carried
to its highest point shortly after Locke's time by John
Law, who thought that credit also had the same functions, and conceived that by increasing credit money, he
really increased the capital of the country. He de-
fended his position in the following manner: "Internal
commerce depends on money; a greater quantity employs more individuals than a smaller quantity. A
limited sum can put to work only a proportionate number of individuals; and it is with little success that laws
are made to employ the poor and idle in a country
where money is scarce. Good laws can carry money
to the highest degree of circulation of which it is sus-
ceptible, and compel it to employ those who are more
profitable to the country; but no law can go farther,
and a larger number of individuals can not be made to
work without a greater quantity of money put in circulation to pay the wages of this large number. It is
possible to lead them to work by credit, but not unless
credit has a sufficient circulation to furnish the needs of
the laborers; on this hypothesis, credit is money, and
produces the same effects as money upon commerce both
internal and external." [2] Upon such principles as these
Law founded his celebrated banking system.

As to the cause of value, Law's statement was founded
chiefly on Locke, but he substituted the term demand
for "vent". He says: "Things draw great value from
the uses to which they are applied; and their value is
greater or less, not so much by reason of their uses,

[1] Quoted by Bauer in Palgrave's Dictionary.

[2] Considérations sur le numéraire et le commerce. Daire, Economistes
Francais du XVIII Siécle, p. 427.

more or less esteemed, more or less necessary, as by reason of their greater or less quantity, compared to the demand which is made for them." He illustrates this point by the classic example of water and diamonds. Law does not attach any precise idea to demand, but merely indicates in a general way, that he means by it the quantity desired. He criticised Locke's idea that the value of money is imaginary. This value, he holds, is no more imaginary than any other value derived from other uses, all uses give value by affecting the demand in relation to the supply.[1]

We have now seen that during the sixteenth and seventeenth centuries value was treated of by two classes of persons, moral philosophers and empiricists; by the former as a part of a general system of ecclesiastical or ethical jurisprudence, by the latter as a part of the argument by which some detail of public policy was advocated. The idea of a "true value" was displaced during this period by that of a "natural value", *i. e.*, that value which would exist under conditions of free and equal competition. This was the special work of the philosophers. In the writings of the empiricists the modern conception of value-in-exchange began to take form; it was purchasing power, and goods were seen to have value not absolutely, but in relation to each other. An absolute value, however, still persisted under the name of intrinsic value.

Thinkers during this period directed their attention almost exclusively to phenomena connected with buying and selling, it was through commerce that nations expected to increase their prosperity, hence value was explained almost entirely from conditions of exchange; but before the close of the period the disposition to look

[1] Considérations, etc., p. 427.

at economic phenomena as a whole began to be manifest, and one of the symptoms of it was a tendency to explain value from the standpoint of production as well as from that of exchange. The resulting theories, although some of them appeared sometime before the close of the seventeenth century, logically belong in the next chapter, which deals with the eighteenth century to the year 1776.

CHAPTER III.

VALUE AND ECONOMIC SCIENCE BEFORE 1776.

It has been maintained that political economy came into existence at a certain stage in the development of French and Scotch moral philosophy.[1] We have seen that the ethical jurists, as Grotius and Puffendorf, had treated of value, price, money and interest in connection with justice in contracts, thus giving to the deductions connected with these economic phenomena an organic place in a general system of jurisprudence. Early in the eighteenth century we find Hutcheson, who used Puffendorf as a text book, dividing the lectures upon moral philosophy which he delivered at the University of Glasgow, into four parts. One of these he devoted to jurisprudence, included economics.[2] Adam Smith, who as a student heard the lectures of Hutcheson,[3] followed his master's divisions when he himself became a lecturer on moral philosophy; but in time what he had to say upon economics swelled to such proportions and appeared to him so important, that he gave it to the world in a separate treatise.[4] In the meantime certain French philosophers had developed a system of economics with which Adam Smith had come in contact before he completed his great work, and which represents the first phase of economic science. The advance toward economic science would not have been possible without the work of the empirical writers of the seventeenth century. They brought together the materials

---

[1] Cohn, History of political economy, p. 14.
[2] Hutcheson, A system of moral philosophy, bk. ii, ch. 12.
[3] Hutcheson lectured from 1730 to 1746.
[4] Cannan, Lectures of Adam Smith, p. xxvi.

of economic history which, with their reflections upon them, could be worked over, and general principles thus deduced, which could be coördinated into a systematic body of knowledge.

In this general process such work as that of Sir William Petty, who is often called the father of statistics, was of great importance. It led to more careful analysis and to the employment of more systematic methods of investigation. But Petty's object was practical rather than theoretical, and his great service was to show what knowledge can be gained from the careful collection and collation of facts. His method, as he himself explained, was to express himself "in terms of *number*, *weight* or *measure;* to use only arguments of sense, and to consider only such causes, as have visible foundations in nature; leaving those that depend upon the mutable minds, opinions, appetites, and passions of particular men to the consideration of others."[1] He therefore devoted himself to such subjects as are now commonly the object of statistical enquiry. In his writings we find conceptions which were to play a fundamental part in the "new economics" of the eighteenth century. For this reason we consider his views upon value in this chapter, where they seem logically to belong, rather than in the last, before those of Barbon, where a chronological order would place them.

In Petty's view, land is the original source of all things constituting wealth, but labor is required to draw them forth from the soil, and additional labor to render them suitable to the uses of man. Hence he says, or rather quotes, "Labor is the father and active principle

[1] Preface to first essay on political arithmetic, (1676), ; ed. Hull, vol. I, p. 244. See also Bevan, Sir William Petty, p. 89, Publications of the American Economic Association, vol. ix, No. 4.

of wealth, as lands are the mother ".[1]   But he does not place the emphasis upon the office of land that it afterwards receives at the hands of the Physiocrats ; his emphasis is rather upon labor, which can overcome natural disadvantages.   But he is so far a mercantilist that he exalts the seaman and trader above the husbandman, because " the following of such trade, which does store the country with gold, silver, jewels, etc., is profitable before others." [2]

Petty's conception of value includes value in exchange or price, and natural value.   He speaks of value in exchange sometimes as extrinsic or accidental value[3] in distinction from intrinsic value, which apparently is the same as natural value.   Again he distinguishes between the intrinsic and extrinsic causes of " dearness and cheapness." [4]   The former are the inner qualities or virtues of the thing, as the " weight, extent, color and clearness" of diamonds.[5]   The latter are what produce fluctuations in supply and demand.   He has some notion of what in modern times has been called normal value.   He considers that a rough estimate of the extrinsic value of land might be made by taking the average of all bargains made within a definite period of time.[6]   Petty recognizes that need affects price ; " as great need of money heightens exchange, so doth great need of corn raise the price of that likewise." [7]   He also appreciates the influence of taste.   He says " opinion of unexampled effects do adde and take away

[1] Taxes and contributions, ch. x ; Petty's Economic writings, ed. Hull, vol. 1, p. 68.
[2] Political arithmetic, (1676), *Ibid.*, p. 260.
[3] Taxes and contributions, ch. 5 ; *Ibid.*, p. 50.
[4] Dialogue of diamonds ; *Ibid.*, vol. 2, p. 625.
[5] *Ibid.*, p. 625.
[6] Taxes and contributions, ch. 5 ; *Ibid.*, vol. 1, p, 49.
[7] *Ibid.*, p. 48.

from the price of things." [1]   Also, "lands intrinsically
alike near populous places, . . . will not only yield
more rent, . . . but also more years purchase than in
remote places, by reason of the pleasure and honor
extraordinary of having lands there." [2]

Petty conceives the natural value of land and labor
to be derived from the value of what they produce.
Thus the natural rent of land is the value of its surplus
produce.[3]   The natural value of commodities is the
quantity of land and labor which enter into their production.   He deems it a "most important consideration
in political economies, viz. how to make a *par* and
equation between lands and labor, so as to express the
value of anything by either alone." [4]   This he does in
the following manner : "Suppose two acres of pasture-
land inclosed, and put thereinto a weaned calf, which
I suppose in twelve months will become 1 C. heavier in
eatable flesh ; then 1 C. weight of such flesh, which I
suppose fifty days food, and the interest of the value of
the calf, is the value or years rent of the land.   But if
a man's labor for a year can make the said land to yield
more than sixty days food of the same, or of any other
kind, then that overplus of days food is the wages of
the man ; both being expressed by the number of days
food." [5]   The day's food Petty regards as a common
measure of value, he reduces it to a unit in the following manner—"That some men will eat more than
others is not material, since by a day's food we understand $\frac{1}{100}$ part of what 100 of all sorts and sizes will
eat, so as to live, labor and generate.   And that a day's

[1] Taxes and contributions, ch. xiv, Petty's Economic writings, ed.
Hull, vol. 1, p. 90.

[2] *Ibid.*, vol. 1, p. 49.

[3] *Ibid.*, vol. 1, p. 43.

[4] The political anatomy of Ireland, *Ibid.*, vol. 1, p. 181.

[5] *Idem.*

food of one sort, may require more labor to produce, than another sort, is also not material, since we understand the easiest gotten food of the respective countries of the world."[1]   A day's food of better quality he regards, as equal to several units, " for one day's delicate and exquisite food may be worth ten of ordinary."[2] Ordinarily however value is not expressed in a day's food but in money, and the quantity of silver which represents the unit, a day's food, is as much as can be produced by the same amount of labor as produced the day's food.   If this quantity changes then the value of commodities in money is altered.   Thus, " if a man can bring to London an ounce of silver out of the earth in Peru, in the same time that he can produce a bushel of corn, then one is the natural price of the other ; now if by reason of new and more easy mines a man can get two ounces of silver as easily as formerly he did one, then corn will be as cheap at ten shillings the bushel, as it was before at five shillings *caeteris paribus.*"[3]

To sum up Petty's theory of value, we may say that he conceived the ultimate source of value, as of wealth, to be land and labor.   By value he meant wealth measured. Hence the natural value of a commodity would be the result of the quantity of land and labor required to produce it.   But its value in the market, its extrinsic value, might vary from the natural value according to the relation of supply to demand.

The English writer who did most at this period to fix in the minds of his countrymen and others, the notion of labor as a measure of value was John Locke, whose work in developing the conception of exchange value we have reviewed.   His interpretation of value

[1] The political anatomy of Ireland, Petty's Economic writings, ed. Hull, vol, 1, p. 181.   [2] *Ibid.*, p. 183.
[3] Taxes and contributions ch. 5 ; *Ibid.*, p. 50.

as derived from labor is needed to complete our view of
his theory as a whole. It was not given in the last
chapter because there we were dealing not only with
the conception of exchange value in itself, but with the
notions that naturally grew up in connection with it in
an age when thought, in seeking causes for the amount
of that exchange value, went little behind the circumstances of the market. In that age the office of labor or
cost was neglected, and its resurrection toward the end of
the seventeenth century marks the beginning of a new
period in the evolution of the theory of value. As is
often the case with original thinkers, Locke not only
gave the best expression to the thought of the period
that was ending, but played an important part in determining the direction of thought in that which was
beginning.

In considering Locke's thoughts on value we must
remember that they were brought in incidentally, as
means to the elucidation of other subjects, so that much
of what he might have said had he been constructing a
theory of value is left to be supplied by the context
and the intelligence of the reader. Locke asserts that
although both land and labor unite in the production
of wealth, "labour makes the greatest part of the value
of the things we enjoy in this world." "Bread, wine
and cloth," he says, "are things of daily use, and great
plenty; yet notwithstanding, acorns, water, and leaves,
or skins, must be our bread, drink and clothing, did
not labor furnish us with these more useful commodities; for whatever bread is more worth than acorns,
wine than water, and cloth or silk than leaves, skins or
moss, that is wholly owing to labour and industry."
But it is not merely the labor that made the commodity
which must be considered but also the labor that pro-

duced tools. "The labour of those who broke the
oxen," he says, "who digged and wrought the iron and
stones, who felled and framed the timber employed
about the plough, mill, oven, or any other utensils,
which are a vast number, requisite to this corn, from
its being seed to be sown to its being made bread, must
all be charged on the account of labour." "It would
be a strange catalogue of things," he continues, "that
industry provided and made use of about every loaf of
bread, before it came to our use, if we could trace them :
iron, wood, leather, bark, timber, stove, bricks, coal,
lime, cloth, dying drugs, pitch, tar, masts, ropes, and
all the material made use of in the ship, that brought
any of the commodities made use of by any of the workmen, to any part of the work ; " he wisely adds, "all
of which it would be almost impossible, at least too
long, to reckon up." And in contrast to this, "The
ground which produces the materials," he says, "is
scarce to be reckoned in." He regards it as a constant
element, so that "it is labour indeed that puts the difference of value on everything." [1]

Locke does not mean what he elsewhere calls "intrinsic" value when he speaks of labor putting value
on things, but rather a kind of exchange value. He
says : "An acre of land, that bears here twenty bushels
of wheat, and another in America, which with the same
husbandry, would do the like, are, without doubt, of
the same natural intrinsic value : but yet the benefit
mankind receives from the one in a year, is worth 5 *l.*
and from the other possibly not worth a penny, if all
the profit an Indian received from it were to be valued,
and sold here ; at least, I may truly say, not one

[1] Essay on civil government (London, 1772) pp. 208, 209, 210.

thousandth." [1] In the essay upon the rate of interest
we have seen that he defined intrinsic value, or "the
intrinsic natural worth of any thing," as consisting in
its fitness to supply the necessities or serve the conveniences of human life ; " [2] this conception is similar
to that of Adam Smith when he defines value, in one
sense, as the utility of some particular object [3] Also in
the same essay we have seen that Locke considered the
"marketable value" of a commodity to be determined
by the proportion of its quantity to its vent, but he
says nothing of the conception of value as determined
by labor.   From this it would seem that when he presented this conception in his essay on government, he
was not thinking of the relative quantities in which
commodities exchange for each other in actual transactions—the problem he had before him in the work on
interest—but of the rule according to which they must
in the long run exchange for each other.   In other
words he had in mind what English economists afterwards defined as natural or normal value.

If we compare the concept of value of Locke and
Petty with that of Barbon, we perceive the main
difference to be that the first is objective and value is
thought of primarily as the attribute of a thing, while
the other is subjective and value is thought of as
emanating from a mind.   This difference represents two
methods which, thus even before political economy became a science, began to characterize the researches of
thinkers.   One method is mechanical, and value is
made to appear as the result of a combination of external conditions ; the other is psychological, and the

[1] *Ibid.*, p. 209.
[2] Works, vol. 2, p. 28.
[3] The wealth of nations, bk. i, ch. 5.

source of value is the mind, external conditions affecting it only as they affect the mind.[1] The germs of
both methods, as we have seen, existed in the middle
ages and are indicated by the the tendency of some
writers to look to market conditions and of others to
to look to utility for the source of value.

In spite of the liberal thought of Petty, Locke,
Barbon and many others it was not in England but in
France that the infant economic science was cradled.[2]
Both the character of philosophical thought and the
economic conditions of the century were more particularly favorable to the appearance in that country of
thinkers who would devote themselves especially to the
construction of an economic science. Mercantilism,
which had for its aim the development of national
prosperity by means of a favorable balance of trade,
had necessarily resulted in an energetic governmental
regulation of commerce and industry, which was carried
out in France under the additional stimulus of the need
of revenue produced by the ambitious policy of Louis
XIV. After the time of Colbert, the management of
the finances fell into the hands of less capable ministers,
and the mercantile policy was less consistently followed ;
but the taxation which remained was of the kind to
stifle that enterprise and thrift which, under other conditions, motives of self interest would have insured.
As a result the agricultural population was impoverished,
public finances were in a most unsound condition, the
manufactures, which Colbert had built up, began to fall
into ruin, and commerce ceased to be carried on with
its former energy.

Boisguillebert, a magistrate of Normandy, contended

[1] Compare Zuckerkandl, Theorie des Preises, pp. 29, 34.
[2] Jevons, Richard Cantillon, *Contemp. R.* 39 : 80.

against Colbertism, especially against the overestimate of the precious metals. He showed that the falling off of the wealth of the kingdom was due to the failure of agriculture, as a result of burdensome and badly adjusted taxation.[1] Marshal Vauban, holding many of the same ideas, recommended a reform in taxation by which a tenth of the agricultural produce should be paid into the public treasury and also a tenth of the incomes derived from trade and manufactures.[2] Other financial reforms were proposed and some of them adopted, but all to no purpose ; they were either inadequate or, like that of Law, only added to the general confusion. Industrial life continued to be in a state of depression, although here and there were signs of recovery ; but gross poverty remained everywhere in striking contrast with the extravagant affluence of the privileged classes. In the meantime, across the channel, English gentlemen were trying experiments upon their estates and adopting new methods of agriculture which were followed by most satisfactory results. Reports of these improvements created quite a sensation in France and were adopted by many landed proprietors, among them the royal physician, François Quesnay.

In order that writers on political and economic subjects should begin consciously to construct a science, it was necessary that they should believe that the acts of men are governed by general principles, that natural law applies in human as well as in physical relations. This point was reached in philosophical thought by Hume, whose essays were translated into French in 1754. He believed in the science of human nature as

---

[1] Le Detail de la France, Daire, Économistes financiers du xviiie Siècle, p. 171.

[2] Dime Royale, Daire, *Op. cit.*, p. 31.

an experimental science, and that general principles must be admitted in judging of human affairs. "General principles" he said, "if just and sound, must always prevail in the general course of things, though they may fail in particular cases; and it is the chief business of philosophers to regard the general course of things." [1] Also in another place, "What depends upon a few persons is, in a great measure, to be ascribed to chance, or secret and unknown causes: what arises from a great number, may often be accounted for by determinate and known causes." [2]

The physiocrats, or economists as they called themselves, believed that the social order, like the physical order, was presided over by natural laws. It followed, therefore that if man by his reason could find out these laws and would obey them, happiness would be assured. To Quesnay and his followers the principle of self interest seemed a sufficient surety for this obedience. The task that these philosophers set themselves, therefore, was to discuss, explain, and propagate the knowledge of laws appertaining to life in society. The physiocrats did not consider natural laws as relations of cause to effect; what they had in mind was a definite order of things necessary to the greatest happiness or well-being of society. Quesnay explains that natural laws are both physical and moral, the physical laws are "the regular course of all the physical events of that natural order which is plainly the most advantageous to mankind," the moral laws are "the rules of all human action of the moral order which conforms to the physical order that is obviously the most advantageous to mankind." [3] Together these are the natural laws upon

---

[1] Essays, Literary, moral and political, London, 1870, p. 150.
[2] *Ibid.*, p. 63. See also Bonar, *Op. cit.*, p. 105.
[3] Le Droit Natural, Oeuvres de Quesnay, ed. Onken, p. 375.

which positive laws should be founded in order to form the most perfect government.[1] This conception is more closely related to that held by Grotius and Puffendorf than to the modern scientific conception of natural law; it was conducive to the building up of a science of economics not only because it introduced general principles into the realm of human action, which was not altogether new, but because it connected human well-being with external nature. The physiocrats believed that they were developing a science of human nature or a general social science. But the principles and phenomena of this science as presented by them were mainly economic, that is, social science with them was in its fundamental principles economics. Thus instead of creating sociology they created political economy.

The fundamental economic postulate of the physiocrats was that the cultivation of the soil is the sole source of new wealth, and alone gives a net income. Thus they differed from Locke and Petty, who derived wealth not only through the agency of agricultural labor but also through that of industrial labor. This doctrine was put forth as early as 1732 by Richard Cantillon in an essay upon commerce to which Quesnay acknowledged indebtedness.[2] Cantillon was of French extraction though born in Ireland and was for several years a merchant and banker in London. Both he and the physiocrats after him regarded money as wealth only in the sense in which other commodities are wealth, *i.e.*, by being useful to man; but its use was only as a medium of exchange, it created no new wealth. Hence there could be no advantage in the so-

---

[1] For an excellent account of the ideas of the physiocrats on these points, see Schelle, Du Pont de Nemours, p. 48, *et seq.*

[2] Grains, Oeuvres, ed. Onken, p. 218.

called favorable balance of trade.   The physiocrats, developing their doctrine further, maintained that manufacture and trade were sterile industries, in that they created no new wealth, but merely changed its form and carried from one place to another that already created. Accordingly they divided society into three classes : the productive class consisting of the cultivators ; the proprietary class consisting of the owners of the soil ; and the sterile class consisting of all others, including public servants.   The first class obtained all new wealth at first hand, out of which it retained only enough to repay it for its services and to replace its capital, and paid the balance or net income to the proprietary class.   The sterile class obtained through exchange its share of the new wealth, which amounted merely to payment for its services from the other two.   This theory of distribution was based upon two cardinal principles, private ownership of land, and freedom of exchange, the realization of which the physiocrats insisted was necessary for a just distribution of wealth and for the well-being and happiness of society.   Therefore they advocated the removal of all restrictions upon industry and especially upon commerce, and urged that the revenue for the government be raised by a single tax upon the net income derived from land.   Such in outline were the fundamental principles of the first school of political economy.   We have now to see what was its theory of value, and how this theory was related to the doctrines of the school as a whole.   We shall begin with Cantillon who has been regarded as a forerunner of the physiocrats.[1]

---

* [1] On Cantillon see Jevons, *Contemp. R.*, vol. 39, p. 61 ; Bauer in *Quart. Journ. of Economics*, vol. 5, p. 100 ; Higgs, Physiocrats, p. 17, *et seq.*

Cantillon[1] points out that some land is more productive than other land, that garments made of the same
quantity and quality of yarn but with different amounts
of labor command different prices; whence he concludes
that "the quantity of the product of the earth, and the
quantity as well as the quality of labor, enter necessarily
into the price." He then develops this proposition by
further examples. A pound of fine lace may be made
at Brussels by the labor of four persons for one year or
of one person for four years. "One sees that the price
which is given for this lace is sufficient to pay for the
subsistence of one person for four years, and to pay in
addition the profits of all the undertakers who deal in
it." In the case of a watch-spring of fine steel the
quality of the labor makes almost the entire value of
the spring. But on the other hand the price of hay and
wood is regulated according to the quantity of the product, that is, according to the fertility of the land which
producéd it. "The price of a cup of water of the river
Seine is nothing, because there is an immense supply
that never dries up; but one gives a sol for it in the
streets of Paris, that is the price or the measure of the
labor of carriage." He then sums up as follows: "By
these inductions and examples, I think it will be understood that the price, or the intrinsic value of a thing, is
the measure of the quantity of land and of the labor
which enters into its production, regard being had to
the fertility or quantity of product of the land, and to
the quality of the labor." From this it is evident that
Cantillon regarded value as fundamentally a relation in
which things stand to what is required to produce them,
and that he considered that any one estimating the real
value of things would estimate it according to what they

[1] Essai sur le commerce, ch. 10.

had cost. He uses the term price to express this cost, he also uses it to express what is given for the thing in the market, what it costs the buyer. The two prices do not necessarily correspond, but they will do so, he thinks, under normal conditions, the latter tending to gravitate to the former.

Thus he continues: things do not always exchange in the market at their intrinsic value. The fancies and tastes of men may be a cause of this. Thus when a gentleman, who at great expense makes a fine garden for his own enjoyment, finally offers it for sale, he will not get half he laid out upon it, unless many long for it; in that case he may get double. The state of consumption also may cause a variation between intrinsic and market value. Thus when farmers raise more corn than is needed, the price " at the market will necessarily fall below the price or intrinsic value." " There is never a variation in the intrinsic value of things; but the impossibility of proportioning in a state the production of merchandise and food to their consumption, causes a daily variation, a perpetual flow and reflow in the market price. Nevertheless in a well-regulated society, the market price of food and merchandise of which the consumption is sufficiently constant and uniform, does not differ much from the intrinsic value; and when it does in years of unusual dearth or superabundance, the magistrates of the town are always in a position to fix the market price of many things, such as bread and meat, so no one need complain."[1]

Carrying his analysis of cost value still farther, he endeavors to find a fundamental cause and measure of the value of labor. " The earth is the material," he says, " labor the form of all food and merchandise ; and

[1] Essai, pp. 38, 39.

as those who work necessarily need to subsist on the products of the earth, it seems that one might be able to find a relation between the value of labor and that of the products of the earth."[1]   Accordingly by a discussion of the needs and habits of different kinds and ranks of workers, and of the needs for bringing up children, he shows that the value of each man's labor corresponds to the quantity of the products of the earth that he requires for his subsistence and for that of his children, or more exactly for double his own subsistence; and the value of each woman's labor corresponds to her own subsistence.   A subsistence, although seen to vary according to the kind of labor, as, for example, farm labor or artisan, and according to the customs of different countries, is still to Cantillon a pretty definite measure, so that in a given country it is possible to form an equation between land and labor, and to state the real or intrinsic value of anything in terms of land only.[2]   Accordingly he says in the introduction to his chapter on trade : " we have tried to prove in the preceding part that the real value of all things of use to man is their proportion to the quantity of land employed for their production, and for the subsistence of those who have given them form."[3]

Cantillon does not agree with Locke that the market price of things in money depends on the proportion between their quantity and the quantity of money in circulation, because it is always possible to alter the

---

[1] Essai, p. 39.

[2] *Ibid.*, ch. II.   Cantillon remarks upon the importance which Petty attached to such an equation, but criticises the latter's investigation " as odd and remote from the laws of nature because it is not concerned with causes and principles but only with effects ; as Locke and d'Avenant and all the English authors who have written something on this matter have done after him." Pp. 54, 55.

[3] Essai, p. 151.

quantity of things by transporting those that are super-abundant. But he thinks Locke's idea just in the sense that the market price is fixed by the proportion of the supply to the demand, *i. e.*, as he seems to mean, the quantity of things and the quantity of money repre-senting the supply and the demand respectively. "In general," he repeats, "market prices do not vary very much from the intrinsic value."[1]

The leader of the physiocrats, Quesnay, did not be-stow upon the analysis of value the special attention which he devoted to other topics; he does not seem at first to have appreciated, as Cantillon certainly did, the place and importance of such an analysis in the construc-tion of economic science. Yet underlying and running through the more purely economic parts of his system, such as the explanation of the sources of wealth, of the primitive and annual advances necessary to insure the greatest possible annual increase of wealth, of the classes of society and the distribution of this annual increase to the members of these classes, there is an implied theory of value which is unmistakable and of such consequence that its content has been held to constitute one of the "truly great scientific achievements" of the physiocratic school.[2] Fundamentally it is like that of Cantillon; but Quesnay makes an important distinction which Cantillon did not make, though it had been made by Locke, namely, the familiar distinction between value in use and value in exchange, (*valeur usuelle*, and *valeur venale*). "The savages of Louisiana," he says "enjoyed a quantity of goods, such as water, wood, game, fruits of the earth, etc., which were not wealth because they had no exchange value. But since some

[1] Essai, p. 157.
[2] Cohn, History of political economy, p. 27.

branches of commerce have been established among them
. . . . . . a part of these goods have acquired an exchange value and have become wealth."[1] Thus it is
exchange value that turns the products of the soil into
wealth, and therefore it is with exchange value alone
that the physiocrats consider political economy to be
concerned. Le Trosne, one of the apostles of the school,
gives the following explanation and definition. "In
society then products acquire a new quality, which
comes from the intercourse of men: this quality is
value, which makes the products wealth . . . . Value
consists in the ratio of exchange which is found between
such things and such other things, between such measure of one product, and such measure of others."[2] By
saying that value makes products wealth, the physiocrats did not mean that what determines value therefore
produces wealth, for nothing could produce wealth that
did not bring forth new matter or substance. Value
was merely the means of measuring wealth, or the ther-
mometer of the wealth and property of the country.[3]
Thus, as between two nations, the state whose goods have
the higher exchange value is the richer.[4]

As to what determines the amount of value, Quesnay
does not make the distinction drawn by Cantillon between intrinsic and market value, but he discusses value,
(*valeur venale*) both from the point of view of exchange,
and from that of production. From the former,
Quesnay considers that value though brought to light in
the market is not at all determined by the personal
circumstances of buyers and sellers. "Prices," he says,
"are not subject to the interests of either buyers or

[1] Notes sur les maximes, Oeuvres, p. 353.
[2] De l'interest sociale, Daire, Physiocrates, p. 889.
[3] *Ibid.*, p. 901.
[4] Quesnay, Questions intéressantes, Oeuvres, p. 299.

sellers; these interests themselves are in reciprocal opposition in the sale and in the purchase; thus the seller
and the buyer considered separately, are not at all the
arbiters of the prices of products. . . . No one is
ignorant that in regard to products, the general cause of
their current price is their scarcity or their abundance,
or the competition more or less great of sellers or of
buyers; and that by these causes the actual price of
products precedes their sale, even that at first hand."
Thus though ascertained by exchange, value and price
are a resultant of general causes existing before the
newly produced wealth is brought into the market.
These general causes lie, in Quesnay's opinion, in the
relation that the consumption of a community bears to
its production. If the former is relatively great, values
and prices will be high. High values, Quesnay maintains, are a great benefit to the people, because by
showing that the products of the soil are extensively
desired they encourage greater reproduction. Thus he
declares in one of his maxims : " Abundance and cheapness is not wealth. Dearth and dearness is poverty.
Abundance and dearness is opulence." [1] The latter
condition would indicate a large consumption as well as
a large production.

Regarding value from the side of production Quesnay
sees as its cause the labor cost which is measured in
the subsistence of the workmen. " If you compare the
gain of the workmen who make the works of industry,"
he says, " with that of the workmen employed in the
culture of the soil, you will find that the gain on both
sides is limited to the subsistence of the workmen ;
that this gain is not an increase of wealth ; and that
the value of the works of industry is in proportion to

[1] Oeuvres, p. 335.

the very value of the subsistence that the workmen and merchants consume. Thus the artisan destroys as much subsistence as he produces by his labor."[1] Upon the same reasoning the gain of the merchant or trader is but a reimbursement for his necessary subsistence, therefore in an exchange there is only an exchange of equal value for equal value and no increase of wealth.[2] The measure of the wealth annually renewed by a nation, is the value of the sale of the produce of the soil at first hand.[3]

Le Trosne, who attempts to elaborate the thought of his master, draws a distinction between value at first hand and subsequent value. The first is the value that the produce of the soil has in the hands of the actual cultivators. The second is that which is added to the produce by subsequent labor. It is by the first alone that the increase of wealth is measured. The difference between the two is determined by the labor, measured by the subsistence that has been expended in changing the form of original wealth or in transporting wealth from one place to another.[4] He names as causes of value: first, utility, which he shows is essential in order that a thing may have value, but he takes pains to point out that utility is not a measure of value; second, the indispensable costs because if expenses are not made good there would be no motive to continue production, and reproduction would not be assured; third, the state of supply, whether the thing be scarce or abundant; fourth, the competition of consumers and products offered for sale. This he considers the sovereign force which decides the value. The amount of

---

[1] Graines, Oeuvres, p. 233.
[2] Oeuvres, p. 386.
[3] Analyse du tableau economique, Oeuvres, p. 307.
[4] De l'interest sociale, Daire, p. 903.

consumption, he points out, depends not only upon the
numbers of the people, but upon the state of comfort
that they enjoy. Since this is chiefly determined by
the amount of the annual production, the production
itself is therefore in Le Trosne's mind the ultimate
cause of value. It decides how much the people are
able to pay for what they buy.[1]

In brief the position of Quesnay and his followers
seems to be that the exchange value of raw material
when it passes from the hand of the cultivators of the
soil who produce it, or "at first hand," is determined by
the relation of its consumption to its production, that
the exchange value of finished goods includes in addition, the value of what the worker has consumed in
living while changing the form of the raw material. As
the consumption in both cases is regarded as repre-
senting the cost of the production, cost is the ultimate
cause and measure of value.

To the orthodox physiocrat, value was cost made
manifest in a rate of exchange predetermined by the
condition of things, *i. e.*, by the actual production compared with the necessary consumption. Hence the
statement that in exchange equal value is given for equal
value, as often reiterated by them, was a mere truism, for
if the cost determined the rate of exchange, things would
exchange in proportion to costs. The doctrine was not
a new one, as we have seen. The canonists believed
that whenever prices were just, equal value was exchanged for equal value. The common mercantilist
opinion that if one party gains in an exchange the other
loses, considered in connection with the distinction between real or intrinsic value and market value, involved
the same conception. For if goods were exchanged at

[1] De l'interest sociale, p. 890, *et seq.*

their intrinsic or cost values, neither party would gain or lose, since values would be equal. But market value which was greater or less than intrinsic value, permitted one side to gain, while the other lost, an amount equal to the difference. The orthodox physiocrats disregarded temporary variations in value. They kept in view only normal exchange value determined by cost. Therefore they announced this proposition as a general principle and drew from it the conclusion that foreign commerce although of some benefit to a nation, was not of great importance. Far from increasing the wealth of a country, it was merely an expense.[1] They advocated freedom of exchange, but they desired the development of internal rather than foreign commerce.

The theory of value held by Quesnay and his followers was the logical companion of their imperfect conception of wealth. They saw that all things which are used by man come originally from the earth, that is, are "gifts of nature." They also recognized that the only motive for industry of any kind is the necessity of procuring things capable of satisfying the wants of man. But they did not put these two facts together, or understand their relation to each other. When Le Trosne said that value is the quality that makes products wealth,[2] he doubtless meant that the degree to which products are wealth is indicated by their value; but he offered no adequate explanation of this truth. Those "gifts of nature" which have value are wealth, because value is the social expression of that usefulness which furnishes the motive for industry. This fact physiocrats like Quesnay and Le Trosne never really comprehended. They recognized value in use, but con-

[1] Quesnay, Oeuvres, p. 286.
[2] *Ante*, p. 86.

sidered it of no importance in economics
acknowledged utility to be a necessary c
value, but saw no connection between utili
amount of value. They therefore failed to
amount of wealth is dependent upon the amount of
utility that is embodied in material things, and that
labor other than the cultivation of the soil, by creating
new utility must produce wealth.

The best exposition of physiocratic theory was made
by Turgot, who, not liking its dogmatic tendencies, re-
fused to identify himself with the school. Nevertheless
his thought was essentially the same upon all points
which the physiocrats considered fundamental. His
treatment of value, however, differs from theirs, not so
much in its final outcome, as because he has developed
it psychologically while the method of Cantillon and
the school of Quesnay is mechanical. They explain
value by causes which are conceived as working of
themselves apart from any effect on the mind and
feelings of people. Turgot, on the other hand, sees in
value the effect of external conditions acting through
human feelings. Indeed, throughout his systematic
treatment of political economy he does not lose sight of
the psychological element, yet he is unable to break
away entirely from the materialism of the physiocrats.
Turgot, however, was not alone in his time in developing a theory of value upon psychological grounds. He
acknowledged indebtedness to Galiani, Abbot of Naples,
whose work[1] upon money should be regarded as belonging in line with the works of Davanzati and
Montanari, though occupying a position much in advance.

Galiani had placed himself in opposition to the

---

[1] Della Moneta, Scrittori classici Italiani di economia politica, parte
moderna, tomo, iii and iv. The work was first published in 1750.

physiocrats in a controversy upon the commerce in grain claiming that they were too absolute in their conclusions as to freedom of trade. His object in writing the book referred to, was to show that money gets its value not from the convention of society, but just as any other commodity gets its value. This led him to explain the cause of value in general. He derives it from the desire for satisfaction inherent in the heart of man. He says, "One can, I believe, say that esteem or value is an idea of proportion between the possession of one thing and the possession of another in the conception of a man."[1] This proportion is an equality between two things, so that a man careful not to have his enjoyments frustrated, exchanges one for another and there is neither loss nor gain. Thus value according to Galiani depends not only upon the feeling we may have about a thing, but also upon a comparison between this feeling and the feeling we may have for something that must be given for it. He fails to see, however, that in this case it is inconsistent to say that in an exchange there is neither loss nor gain, for both parties must gain. Yet the conception of the dependence of value on human feeling is very plain in his thought. He shows that since human dispositions vary, the values of things vary. On the one hand, there are the things generally sought which have what one may call current value. Other things draw their value from the individual desire of those who covet them and of those who give them up. Value, he maintains, is a composite conception and can be analyzed by a calculus of utility and scarcity. Air and water have no value because they have no scarcity. A bag of sand from the beaches of Japan would be rare,

[1] Della Moneta, libro i, page 58.

but would be of no value because it would have no
utility.

He takes up first the calculus of utility. Many
doubt that there can be great utility in some merchandise of great price; therefore it is necessary to explain
utility at length, and the way it is measured. " I call
utility," he says, " the aptitude that a thing has for procuring us happiness." Having noted that we have
other wants and passions besides those of eating, drink-
ing and sleeping, which arise when these are satisfied,
he draws up a classification of goods according to
utility as follows : " In the series of useful things the
first are the elements; then comes man, who, of all
things is the most useful to another man ; then the
things which serve for nourishment, then those which
serve for clothing, then there follows those which serve
for habitation, and in the last place those which serve
as the less important commodities and for the satisfaction of the secondary desires of man." The statements,
" a natural calf is more noble than a golden calf, but
how much less prized," " a pound of bread is more useful than a pound of gold," Galiani calls " shameful para-
logisms," that are due " to ignoring the fact that more
or less useful are relative terms and that their import
corresponds to the different states of persons." Further
on he speaks of the influence of fashion upon value and
upon our ideas, " it has the effect of causing the utility
of things to vary by causing the enjoyment caused by
their use to vary." The value of things unique like
the Venus de Medicis, or products of monopolies, is not
infinite or indefinite, but corresponds to the needs and
desires of the purchaser and the estimation of the seller.
Thus Galiani recognized the personal or subjective
nature of utility and saw that the value of some things

is but the result of a comparison between subjective utilities.

Taking up scarcity Galiani defines it as the proportion existing between the quantity of a thing and the use made of it. Use is not destruction only but such occupation of a thing, that while one person uses it, it cannot satisfy another. Both destruction and the withdrawal of things from commerce can raise the price of those that are left, but the former more than the latter. He next makes a distinction familiar in modern economics, that between goods which can and goods which cannot be reproduced at will. There are two classes of things as to quantity : the first is those whose quantity depends upon nature, as fruits of the earth and animals, the second those which depend upon labor. In analyzing the second class in regard to quantity, one needs to consider only labor, because the quantity is proportional to the labor. In analyzing labor there are three elements to be considered : the number of people employed, the time spent, the different quality of the work. There are some things, as a bale of cloth, whose value is equal to the nourishment of the number of persons employed during the time necessary to finish the work. In an analysis of the time spent, it is necessary to consider the time spent in rest, and also in holidays. If a man work three hundred days in the year and produce one hundred pairs of boots the value of these boots will correspond to his nourishment for one year. If another work three hundred and sixty days and produce one hundred and twenty pairs of boots he can sell them one fifth cheaper than the first, "for he will have no need of drawing from one hundred and twenty pairs of boots a gain superior to that which the first drew from his one hundred pair." Some labors,

by their nature, cannot be practiced continually, as in
the fine arts.   Arts, also which require long apprentice-
ship and impose great expense on parents, are paid
more dearly.   So pine or walnut is dearer than poplar or
elm because of the slowness with which it grows.   The
value of the various talents of man, Galiani thinks, is
governed by the same principles that govern the price
of inanimate things.   Divine Providence has made
the most necessary talents, such as agriculture, the
commonest.   Peasants are as the bread and wine of
men, philosophers as the precious stones.

After this interesting and acute analysis of utility
and scarcity Galiani concludes in the following manner.
" I have now said enough of the principles upon which
value depends; one knows now that these principles
are certain, constant, universal and founded upon order
and the nature of the things of this world, nothing is
arbitrary and fortuitous here below, but all is order,
harmony and necessity.   Values are various but not
capricious.   Their variations even are subject to an
order, to an exact and unchangeable rule.   They are
ideas : but when they are founded upon needs and enjoyments, that is to say upon the internal constitution
of man, our ideas are essentially just and stable."   But
he warns his reader against thinking that value is easily
determined, as might seem after what has been said.
Value cannot be determined *a priori*, for scarcity and
value depend upon consumption, and consumption
varies according to value.   The problem contains two
unknowns and hence is indeterminate.   Price influences
consumption.   Each consumer desires things according
to the inconvenience and labor that their acquisition
costs.   If the inconvenience be great he prefers to use
things having less value.   Consumption is governed by

price which is itself governed by scarcity; in years of bad harvest the price is higher and the consumption less, *i. e.*, a people spend only a fixed amount for corn, which in some years buys more, in others less, according to the harvest. As prices are lowered desires grow. Hence an equilibrium is preserved. Prices tend to seek a level.

Galiani did not think it necessary to distinguish between value in use and value in exchange. What he had in mind, however, was exchange value. The amount of value, he shows, depends upon a combination of utility and scarcity, meaning by the latter supply in relation to demand, but while the precise value cannot be known *a priori*, because each of the two is a variable, the result is not fortuitous but according to law. In this he has given a qualitative rather than a quantitative analysis of the law of value.[1]

Turgot treated of value in two works, in his "Reflections on the formation and the distribution of riches," which was written about 1766, and in an unfinished essay entitled "Value and money,"[2] which according to Daire, was apparently intended for the Dictionary of Commerce projected by the Abbé Morellet.[3] It was written about the same time as the Reflections, and is the more elaborate treatment of the two. In this essay he begins with the etymology of the word *valeur*. It is the substantive of *valoir* which is from the Latin *valere* signifying force, vigor, also to be well. This meaning is retained in the words valid, invalid and con-

---

[1] Della Moneta, libro i, cap. ii. On Galiani see A. Dubois, Les théories psychologiques de la valeur on xviiie siècle, in *Revue d'économie politique*, Sept. and Oct., 1897. The last number contains a translation into French of that part of Galiani's work relating to value. See also Graziani, p. 99.

[2] Valeur et monnaies, Oeuvres, vol. i, p. 75–93.

[3] Daire, Notice historique sur Turgot, Oeuvres, vol. i, p. 45.

valescence. The words *valoir* and *valeur* have in
common usage a sense different from that which they
have in commerce, but which is nevertheless the basis of
the latter. " It (*valoir*) expresses that goodness relative
to our needs by which goods and gifts of nature are
regarded as adapted to our enjoyment, to the satisfaction
of our desires. One says that a stew is worth nothing
when it is bad to the taste. . . . . . The adjectives bad,
mediocre, good, excellent, characterize the different degrees of this kind of value. . . . . . Although this
goodness may be always relative to us, we have nevertheless in view, in explaining the word value, a real
quality, intrinsic to the object and by which it is suited
to our usage." This last statement has been characterized as an " unfortunate phrase in which the author
confounds the conditions with the cause of value," and
stigmatized as being " in formal contradiction with his
theory and with the definition which he assumes." [1]
What Turgot probably meant, however, was that value
is something concrete, not an abstract relation, such as
is implied by the expression, ratio in exchange ; it is a
definite amount of excellence or importance attributed
to the object valued ; but in his desire to make clear the
concreteness of his idea he confused value with utility.

Turgot begins his analysis with the simplest case
imaginable, that of the isolated man. This individual
seeks an object which he judges adapted to his enjoyment, " he will find it good, and this relative goodness
can be absolutely termed value." " But this value, not
being compared with other values, will not be suscept-
ible of measurement, and the thing which has worth
will not be rated " (*evaluée*). Measurement of value or

[1] Dubois, *Rev. d'econ. pol.*, vol. xi, p. 859.

valuation comes with the comparison of objects with
respect to the enjoyment they can give. At first the
isolated man compares only present enjoyments and
thus values things only in relation to present enjoyment; but in the course of time future enjoyments
enter into his calculations, and value is estimated also
in things which, although incapable of contributing to
enjoyment at present, will, if held in possession, do so
at a future time. "Then the man begins to compare
his wants, to proportion the quest of objects not only to
the quick impulse of present wants, but to the order of
necessity and utility of different wants." To the general capacity of a thing for satisfying a present want
Turgot apparently assigns the term excellence, while
he assigns the term utility to the power of a thing to
satisfy a future want. But the order of excellence, he
explains, enters into or modifies the order of utility,
"for the pleasure of the more lively enjoyment which
this degree of excellence produces is itself an advantage
which man compares with the greater urgency of the
things of which he prefers an abundance to the excellence of a single one." The necessity of providing for
future wants and the sentiment of present need are two
considerations upon which the isolated man bases his
estimation of value. A third consideration is "the
greater or less difficulty which man faces in procuring
the object of his desire, for it is very evident that, between two things equally useful and equally excellent,
that which requires more trouble to acquire appears to
him much more precious, and he will employ more
care and effort to procure this thing for himself."
"This is the reason why water in spite of its usefulness
is not regarded as precious in the country where it
abounds, ... but in the desert it has an infinite

price." Thus even before we come to exchange we find scarcity an element in valuation. Turgot here uses scarcity as another name for difficulty of attainment, and makes a somewhat equivocal attempt to reduce the conception to that of utility. " It is necessary to remark, " he says, " that this esteem attached to scarcity is again founded on a particular kind of utility, because it is more useful to provide one's self in advance with a thing difficult to obtain than with one more choice, and man makes more effort to appropriate the former." These three considerations, namely, the sense of present need, the necessity of providing for future wants, and the difficulty of attainment, or excellence, utility and scarcity, "are all," says Turgot, " which enter into the determination of the kind of value that is relative to isolated man." " To designate it," he continues, " by a suitable name we shall call it estimative value (*valeur estimative*), because it is in effect the expression of the degree of esteem which man attaches to the different objects of his desire."

Thus far Turgot's analysis has been qualitative. He has shown that value arises out of the desires of man which are proportional to one another, occupying different places in a scale of values. He now wishes to discover what determines the amount of each particular value, or the measure of value, in the case of the isolated man. This measure he finds to be " labor, the employment of his faculties and time," which man must pay in a primary commerce with nature to obtain the objects of his desire. Difficulty of attainment as one of the causes of estimative value has thus far figured as one incentive of desire, " that which he will have more trouble to obtain appears to him more precious, etc." ; now this necessary trouble appears as the measure

or denominator of value, the price paid for the object
in a primary commerce with nature. The valuation
which he has put upon the object because of its importance to his well-being, what is it but " the account
which he renders to himself of that portion of his labor
and his time, or to express these two things in a single
word, of that portion of his faculties which he employs
in the quest of the object valued, without sacrificing to
it the quest of other objects equally or more important ?"
The unit of the scale of comparison of values is then
the sum total of a man's faculties, and each valuation
is a fraction of this unit. "It is precisely the portion
of the total of his faculties which responds to the desire
which he has for the object, or which he is able to employ to satisfy the desire. . . . One may say, in other
terms, that it is the ratio of that proportional part to
the total of the faculties of man, a ratio which would
be expressed by a fraction which would have
for numerator one of the numbers representing the
values or the equal proportional parts that make up the
total of the faculties of the man." If these numbers
were 1, 2, 3, 4, 5, etc., up to 100, then the valuation of
a particular object of desire would be expressed by .01,
.02 or .03, etc., according to the proportional part of his
faculties necessary to obtain that object. This ingenious
explanation was inspired by a statement of Galiani
which had impressed Turgot and which he epitomized
by the phrase, "the common measure of all value is
man." Galiani said: "The price of things, that is to
say the proportion existing between things and our
wants, has not yet a fixed measure. Perhaps one may
be found. For my part, I believe that there is no other
but man himself."[1] What Turgot really means is that

---

[1] Dubois, *Rev. d'econ. pol.*, vol. xi, p. 852.

the personal valuation or, to use his own term, the estimative value is determined by that personal sacrifice which the nature of the case requires. No isolated man will be apt to attach a greater importance to the object of his desire than what corresponds to the effort he must make to obtain it. This is a cost theory of value. But the merit of Turgot's explanation is that it shows that cost affects value, by first limiting desire.

Turgot now comes to exchange value. For this part of his exposition he supposes two men cast upon a desert isle in the midst of the northern sea. One has a superabundance of fish, the other a superabundance of skins. They will demand each of the other his surplus in order that the one need not be cold or the other go hungry. Each will give the other what he demands, and thus commerce will be born. What has happened in this case is that the surplus portions of the two commodities, otherwise useless, have acquired a value in the eyes of their possessors which they did not have before; each has placed a value upon that of which he had no personal need. It is probable that in this first situation the debate upon the conditions of exchange will not be very lively; all the surplus fish will be given for all the surplus skins. "But let us change the supposition a little, let us give to these two men an interest in guarding their surplus, a motive for attaching value to it; let us suppose that instead of fish one has brought corn, which can be preserved a long time, and that the other instead of skins has brought fire-wood, and that the isle produces neither grain nor wood." Unfavorable conditions, such as a stormy season, make it impossible for either to return to the continent for more supplies. The man with corn needs wood to keep from freezing, the possessor of wood desires corn that he may not starve. There is great need of exchange, but each one will calculate the force of his needs to determine his interest in keeping that which he has and in acquiring that which he has not. "In a word, he will fix precisely the estimative value of each interest in relation to himself. This estimative value is proportional to the interest that he has in procuring for himself the two things; and the comparison of the two values is evidently only the comparison of the two interests." Each is also animated by the general interest of keeping as much as he can of his thing and of acquiring as much as he can of the other's thing. Each holds in secret his own estimative value and sounds the possessor of the thing he wants by small offers and large demands. "They dispute upon the conditions of exchange, and as both have a great interest in agreeing, they will agree at last." They exchange, let us say, four measures of corn for five armfuls of wood. Each one without doubt places a higher estimative value upon that which he receives than upon that which he gives. This "is essential to the exchange, for it is the sole motive of it. Each one would remain as he was if he did not find an interest, a personal profit, in exchanging." This view of exchange is in agreement with the general physiocratic doctrine that exchange is for the advantage of all who take part, but Turgot was apparently the first to explain it as a gain in value. And even to him it is a gain in estimative value only. This gain is precisely equal on each side he maintains, "for if it were not equal one of the two would desire the exchange less than the other and would force him to come down in his price by making a larger offer. It is then always exactly true that each one gives equal value for equal value."

"Let us see precisely what this exchangeable value

is," Turgot continues. It is not precisely estimative value, for in the determination of estimative value each man separately compared two interests. "In the determination of the exchangeable value there were two men, comparing and four interests compared, but the two interests of each of the two participants have first been compared by them apart, and these are two resultants which are afterwards compared together, or further debated by the two participants, in order to form a mean estimative value which grows into precisely the exchangeable value in question, to which we may give the name appreciative value, (*valeur appreciative*), because it determines the price or the condition of exchange." Appreciative value is of the same nature as estimative value, but differs from it in that it is a mean estimative value. "We have proved that the estimative value of an object for isolated man is no other than the ratio between the portion of his faculties which a man can devote to the quest of this object, and the total of his faculties; then the appreciative value in exchange between two men is the ratio between the sum of the portions of their faculties which they will be disposed to devote to the quest of each of the objects of exchange and the sum of the faculties of the two men." By reducing both estimative value and appreciative value to terms of energy, Turgot has shown how exchange value is but an outgrowth of individual valuations.

Appreciative value, he next points out, is not a ratio between two things exchanged, "or between the price and the thing sold, as some persons have been inclined to think," but it is the value of each of the things compared, which two values are equal. "One must not confuse," he says, "the values which have relation of equality, with this relation of equality which supposes two values compared." Turgot wishes to guard his reader against confusing the thing itself with the mathematical expression of the thing. Appreciative value is a definite attribute of the thing valued, but it may be expressed as a ratio in exchange.

Value cannot be announced by itself, the fraction of energy or human faculty to which a particular value is equal, cannot itself be expressed. The numerator is " a thing inappreciable." Besides in a calculation of these faculties it would be necessary to consider time. Here it is difficult to fix upon a suitable unit or to estimate time in its relation to its many different kinds of employment. Thus while it is impossible to express value in terms of itself, it can be and is announced by price, that is by stating the quantity of what is given for that which is bought, or by saying that a certain quantity of one thing is equal to a certain quantity of another thing in value. Turgot here takes considerable pains to show that that in which the price is expressed is not itself a real measure of value. Although the use of the two words value and price interchangeably is, to be sure, sufficiently exact for the language of commerce, since in every exchange each quantity of the things exchanged serves reciprocally as the price and to express the value of the other, nevertheless those two words express essentially different ideas. The number of aliquot parts of one thing that is given for another thing in exchange no more measures the value of that thing than the ell of France measures the vare of Spain, although the latter may be expressed in terms of the former. Simple as this truth is, Turgot remarks, it has often been misunderstood by very good minds and administrations have been led into error, as

in the case of the famous system of Law. Thus he
would have us understand that although values may be
expressed or denominated in terms of paper money, the
denominations are not measurements of them, they can
only be measured by the human energies necessary to
produce them.

Having thus far explained the fundamental conceptions of value on the simple hypotheses of an isolated
man and two exchangers, Turgot next proceeds to com-
plicate his conditions. He supposes four men instead
of two, but only two things, corn and wood. If these
four men are divided into pairs which are separated
from each other there will be two different appreciative
values, but this will not prevent each man getting an
equal value for equal value given in each case. If the
four men come together and learn these rates of exchange, the conditions of exchange will at once be altered, there will be a new appreciation of the value of
wood and of the value of corn, which will be the same
in the two exchanges and for the four participants.
The same quantity of wood will be given for the same
quantity of corn in each exchange, for "if one possessor of corn would take less wood than the other for
the same quantity of corn, the two possessors of wood
would address themselves to him for the profit of this
reduction." He would then raise his demand for wood,
while the other possessor of corn would lower his.
This would continue until the two possessors of corn
would offer the same quantity for the same quantity of
wood.

At this point the fragment, Value and money, ends.
In the Reflections, which Turgot himself characterized as "a sketchy sort of analysis of the labours of

society and of the distribution of riches,"[1] he does not attempt a lengthy description of estimative and appreciative value, nor does he use these terms. But after a short explanation of the " principle of the valuation of commercial things," he proceeds to show how " the current value establishes itself in the exchange of commodities." The process is the competition of demanders on both sides, and finally "it is fixed by the balance of the wants and abilities of the whole body of the sellers of corn with those of the whole body of the sellers of wine. . . . . . . The price midway between the different offers and the different demands will become the current price, whereto the buyers and sellers will conform in their exchanges."[2]

In comparison with Galiani, Turgot's treatment of value fails in that he has not given so complete and satisfactory an analysis of utility; but while Galiani regards the labor element as affecting value chiefly through its effect upon the element scarcity, Turgot has given it a fundamental position, making it the ultimate measure and determiner not only of exchange value but also of personal or private value. It is notable that he has made no distinction between subjective and objective as applied to value. Both exchange or appreciative value and estimative value are of the same kind, and both are subjective. Turgot is vastly superior to the physiocrats in psychological analysis, but the outcome is not essentially different. In a letter to Hume, he says: "And you justly observe that it is not taxes, high or low, which determine the price of wages, but simply the relation of supply and demand.

[1] Letter to Du Pont, Dec. 9, 1766, Turgot, Econ. classics, 110.
[2] Reflections on the formation and distribution of wealth, Turgot, Econ. classics, §§ xxxi, xxxii.

This principle has certainly never been disputed ; it is the only principle which fixes at the time the price of all the things which have a value in commerce.   But one must distinguish two prices, the current price, which is established by the relation of supply to demand, and the fundamental price, which, in the case of a commodity, is what the thing costs the workman.   In the case of the workman's wages, the fundamental price is what his subsistence costs the workman." [1]

The physiocrats carried on a very active propaganda, the economic reforms which they advocated were presented in every light, the theories upon which they were based were elaborated, and the views of their opponents controverted in numerous articles which appeared upon the pages of their journals [2], or in more extended treatises.   The Abbé de Condillac cannot be ranked as an opponent of the school, yet he exhibited some fundamental differences which are of especial importance in a history of the theory of value.   These appear in a little work upon commerce which he published in 1776. [3]   He agreed with the economists in their main thesis that the soil is the original source of wealth. But he maintained that wealth, in as much as it consists in things that have value, is increased by whatever increases value, that therefore commerce and the arts are capable of increasing wealth. [4]   The basis of this doctrine is the theory of value with which he begins his treatise.   In his view the foundation of value is utility.   Utility is founded upon the need we have for

---

[1] Econ. classics, p. 107.

[2] See Quesnay, Oeuvres, p. 378, *et seq.* ; see also Higgs, The physiocrats, lecture vi.

[3] Le commerce et le gouvernment considéré relativement l'un à l'autre.

[4] *Ibid.*, chs. 6 and 7.

a thing. "According to this utility we esteem it more
or less fit for the uses in which we wish to employ it.
Now this esteem is what we call value. To say that a
thing has worth, is to say that it is good, or that we esteem it good, for some use." He significantly points
out that it is not the utility itself but our knowledge of
the utility of a particular thing that causes it to have
value. "One is inclined," he says, to "regard value as
an absolute quality, which is inherent in things, independent of the judgment we entertain of them, and this
confused notion is a source of bad reasoning. It is
necessary then to remember that, although the things
have a value because they have the qualities which
make them suited to our needs, they will have no value
for us, if we do not judge that they have in fact these
qualities. Their value is then principally in the judgment that we entertain of their utility."

Not only the utility, but the state of the supply of
the things that we need, is a cause of the degree of
esteem which we have for them. This is because "In
abundance, one feels the need less, because one does not
fear a shortage. For an opposite reason one feels it
more in scarcity and in dearth." A need more strongly
felt, gives to a thing a greater value, a need less strongly
felt, a less value. "The value of things increases then
in scarcity, and diminishes in abundance." Also a
need a long way off will give a thing less value than
a present need. Thus "the more or less of value,
utility remaining the same, is founded on the scarcity
of things or on their abundance, or rather on the
opinion that we have of their scarcity or their
abundance. I say *utility remaining the same*, because
it is plain enough, that in supposing them equally rare
or equally abundant, one judges them more or less of

value, according as one judges them more or less useful."
In illustrating these principles Condillac criticises the
opinion that water has no value because "it costs
nothing to procure it; and the value which it obtains
by transport, is not its value, it is the value of the cost
of carriage." "It is very astonishing" he says in
answer, "that one pays the cost of carriage to procure
a thing that is worth nothing, a thing does not have
value because it costs, as one may suppose, but it costs,
because it has value." Cost he regards as consisting
not merely of expense but of labor. Labor he defines
as an action or a continuation of actions for the sake of
obtaining an advantage. Even water at the bank of
the river has value; it also has a cost, namely the action
of kneeling to take it; "an action which is a very
small labor, . . . but then the water has the least possible value." But it is worth the labor performed to
procure it. Condillac views cost, then, as neither the
cause nor the measure of value, but the evidence of it.
He also contends against the idea that a thing can have
value only as it has a certain degree of scarcity. "*A
certain degree of scarcity*. This is just what I do not
mean. I conceive that a thing is scarce, when we judge
that we have not enough of it for our use; that it is
abundant, when we judge that we have more than we
need. In fine, I conceive that a thing of which one
makes   nothing   and   of   which   one   can   make
nothing   has   no   value,   and   on   the   contrary   a
thing has value when it has utility; and if it has not
that by which it is useful, it will not have a greater
value in scarcity and a less in abundance." Condillac's
conception is, in brief, that subjective utility is the
ultimate source of value, while subjective utility made
definite by the urgency of our need, which is itself a

function of scarcity, determines the amount or degree of value. His theory is more consistently psychological than that of either Turgot or Galiani. Neither of these writers realize to the same degree the importance of the psychological reflex [1] from such external conditions as the state of supply, they do not speak in the same pointed way of utility, scarcity, labor, etc., as working through the mind, through human thought and feeling.

Passing to the formation of price, Condillac discusses two cases of exchange. In the first case I exchange my surplus corn for your surplus wine; in the second my surplus is sufficient for you, but your surplus is not enough for me. In this case I will not give you the whole of my surplus for yours, since I want some left to satisfy the balance of my need elsewhere, and you wanting all my surplus will not give all yours for any less. After many reciprocal offers a bargain is struck at valuations which lie between those first made of corn in wine and wine in corn. "When all in general agree to give so much wine for so much corn, then the corn in relation to the wine and the wine in relation to the corn have each a value which will be recognized generally by all." "Now this relative value generally recognized in the exchanges," he continues, "is that which is the foundation of the price of things. The price is then only the estimated value of one thing in relation to the estimated value of another. . . . . The things are reciprocally the price of one another." Further as to the nature of price, "In the first place," he says "the price of things is relative to the estimation that we make of them; or rather it is only the estimation that we make of one in relation to the other, and this is not astonishing, for originally, price and estimation were

[1] Zuckerkandl, Zur Theorie des Preises, p. 45.

words entirely synonymous, and the idea that the former at first signified, is identical with the idea that the second expresses to-day. In the second place, they are reciprocally the price of one another." The words price and value ought not to be used interchangeably. " When we have need of a thing it has value; it has it by that alone, and before there is any question of making an exchange. . . . . . It is only in exchange that it has a price . . . . and its price . . . is the estimation that we make of its value when in exchange we compare its value with the value of another."

The causes of the variations of prices Condillac holds to be first, abundance and scarcity, because they make needs more or less; and second, alterations in the relative quantities of things to one another, or, to use his way of putting it, alterations in the number of people desiring to exchange one thing in relation to the number desiring to exchange another. In an exchange each party thinks that he gives less value for more, otherwise he would not exchange. This would always have been understood if exchanges had always been made without money, for each one would have seen that he gave what was to him a superfluity for what was necessary. But the advantage in exchange is not always equal : one may give of what is a superfluity to him to get what is a necessity, and the other may give of what is a necessity to him to get what is a greater necessity. In this case the former gains more than the latter. The use of money as a common measure of value has led people to think that they exchange equal value for equal value. By this argument, in pointed opposition to the physiocrats and Turgot, Condillac lays the foundation for his theory that wealth is increased by commerce. It was criticised by Le Trosne[1] who maintained with great persistence the doctrine of Quesnay that in buying and selling there is only exchange of equal value for equal value, and that therefore commerce is not instrumental in the production of wealth.

The psychological theories of this period deserve more consideration than they have received.[2] They were attempts to trace economic phenomena to their ultimate sources. They were more profound than any that had yet been offered. But they were incomplete. Turgot saw that the judgment of man is controlled by external conditions and he made cost in terms of energy the ultimate arbiter of value; but, although he did not wholly neglect it, he did not give sufficient weight to the influence of the supply on hand, or the amount of enjoyment already obtained from the consumption of a good, in other words the urgency of the specific want in determining the portion of energy any man would be willing to devote to the acquisition of another good of the same kind. Condillac, on the other hand, neglected the influence of cost upon the judgment estimating utility. Neither saw in all its details the process by which want and provision for want mutually limit each other in determining the personal valuations of buyers and sellers, before they enter the market where an exchange value is finally set upon the good.

The psychological method did not appeal to the orthodox physiocrats. The object of their investigations was after all practical rather than theoretical, they were really seeking measures by which national prosperity could be secured and not the ultimate causes of certain

[1] De l'interest sociale, Daire, p. 905.
[2] For an exposition of these theories see an article in the *Revue d'économie politique*, Sept. 1897, by A. Dubois.

phenomena interesting in themselves as unsolved problems of nature. They did not derive their measures
from general principles already established, but sought
these principles to support the measures. Economic
science did not give birth to the *impôt unique*, and the
policy of freedom of trade, but was itself born because
these proposed reforms needed explanation. They cared
little therefore for the fine-spun theories of the psycholo-
gists. It was proving nothing but what everybody admitted, to show, for example, that utility is a necessary
condition of value. They were prepared by the disposition of the mercantilists to reckon the economic
prosperity of society as one reckons the profit and loss
of a private business. Therefore they preferred the
mechanical explanations of value which derive it either
from cost considered as the expenses of subsistence or
from the relation of demand and supply in the market.
Mechanical theories are usually represented by two
classes of writers whom we may distinguish according
as they give greater weight, in explaining how the
amount of exchange value is determined, to cost or to
demand and supply. The physiocrats emphasized cost.
The writers who emphasize supply or demand are
represented, in this period, by Sir James Steuart, whose
explanation deserves not to be passed over. He was a
native of Scotland but had travelled abroad extensively
and resided for some years in France. There he no
doubt became more or less familiar with the ideas of
the physiocrats. In 1767 he published an elaborate
work entitled " An Inquiry into the principles of political economy." This work can scarcely be ranked as a
treatise upon economic science; it is rather a series of
dissertations upon the different parts of what the author

calls the "domestic policy in free nations." He has been called a moderate mercantilist, and this title best describes him.[1]

Steuart by no means overlooks the element of cost in the determination of value, for he says that in the price of goods there are two things: the real value of the commodity, and the profit upon alienation." When a manufacture comes to be sold, there must be known: 1. "How much of it a person can perform in a day, a week, a month, according to the nature of the work, which may require more or less time to bring it to perfection. . . 2. The value of the workman's subsistence and necessary expense. . . 3. The value of the materials. These three articles being known, the price of the manufacture is determined. It cannot be lower than the amount of all three, that is, than the real value; whatever it is higher, is the manufacturer's profit. This will ever be in proportion to demand, and therefore will fluctuate according to circumstances."[2] This is Steuart's explanation of "how the prices of things are determined by trade." In his treatment of money and coins he enumerates the following principles which determine the value of things. "The value of things depends upon the general combination of many circumstances, which however may be reduced to four principal heads:

1 mo.   The abundance of the things to be valued.

2 do.   The demand which mankind make for them.

3 tio.   The competition between the demanders; and

4 to.   The extent of the faculties of the demanders."

The function therefore of money, he adds, "is to publish

---

[1] Cossa, Introduction etc., p. 234; see also Cunningham, Eng. industry and commerce, vol. ii, p. 429-31; and Zuckerkandl, p. 41.

[2] Inquiry into the principles of political economy, vol. i, pp. 181, 182.

and make known the value of things, as it is regulated by the combination of all these circumstances." [1]

Steuart's treatment of demand is interesting and ingenious. Demand stands to trade as wants to bartering. Demand is relative to merchandise. A ship arriving in port offers, while the port demands; a ship unloaded demands, while the port offers. Demand is simple or compound,—simple when there is no competition of interests demanding, compound when there is such competition. It is great when the quantity demanded is great, small when the quantity demanded is small. It is high when the competition of buyers is great, low when the competition of sellers is great. The consequence of a great demand is a great sale; of a high demand a great price; of a small demand a small sale; of low demand, a low price. Demand encourages industry, and when it is regularly made, the effect of it is that the supply is for the most part in proportion to it. Then demand is simple; but circumstances may make it compound, as when the usual supply unexpectedly fails. The consequence of this is a competition among buyers which raises current or ordinary prices. Whence comes the saying, demand raises prices. Demand affects prices differently according as it is a demand for necessities or things to which people are indifferent; also according as it is a demand made by consumers, or by merchants. Steuart had the same fundamental conception of value as the other writers of his period who treated the subject mechanically. There is a real intrinsic value determined by cost, and a market value determined by the relation of demand to supply, and whether the value is high or low depends upon whether the competition be-

[1] Inquiry, etc., p. 521.

tween buyers or between sellers is the more intense. But his analysis contains little of importance beyond serving to illustrate a mechanical explanation from demand and supply, which is a working out of what had already been suggested by Locke and Law.

CONCLUSION

What now are the main features of the evolution of the theory of value up to the point we have reached? What has been the progress in the conceptions of the nature of value, and in the analyses of the causes which determine the amount of value?

The evolution of the conceptions of the nature of value is marked by two main features : the first is the growth of the conception of exchange value, and the second is the advance of a subjective conception of value. The time honored distinction between value-in-use and value-in-exchange may be safely regarded as inaccurate, for it involves two ideas that are not mutually exclusive. Value-in-exchange is really a kind of value-in-use, to purchase other goods being one way of using a good. A better distinction and one which does not have this objection may be drawn not between two kinds of value, but between two phases of value according to the nature of the valuing subject. If the value is the product of the mental and emotional activity of a single individual one phase is represented, or if it is the common product of the thinking and feeling of many persons constituting a society another phase is represented. These phases may be designated briefly as personal or individual value, and social value, although these terms are not without objection.[1] But the use of the terms

[1] They are used by Wagner, see Lehrbuch, part i, vol. i, p. 329. Prof. Wm. W. Folwell uses the term valuation in the sense here intended for personal value in lectures before his elementary classes.

subjective and objective, which have been suggested, is still more objectionable because social value, although objective to the individual mind, is still subjective to the mind of society.[2] Exchange value, according to the distinction we have made, is but a form of social value, it is the importance that is socially attached to goods because they are able to procure other goods in exchange, it is the purchasing power they are deemed to possess.

We have seen that the conception of exchange value depended upon particular historical conditions. These conditions were two: first, a "money economy," or, better, that state of economy in which goods are produced to sell, and in which each person expects to satisfy his wants by buying and not by making the thing he needs; second, a supreme interest in industrial activities spreading among people generally. The first only of these conditions was realized in ancient Greece and Rome. Among both peoples the conception of exchange value did appear, but because the second condition was wanting it was not made in any general way an object of scientific investigation and discussion. Even Aristotle, whose description of exchange value is the most complete; treated economic phenomena as subordinate to ethical.

During the middle ages neither of these conditions were present. It was a time when the prevailing economy was "natural"; when the social constitution was a system of dependent personal relationships; and economic regulation was the function of small, more or less

---

[2] Dietzel maintains that a distinction between subjective and objective has some point in practical economics which deals with objective fair or just values, but not in theoretical economics which deals with value only as a product of the mind. Theoretische Socialökonomik, p. 212 in Wagner, Lehrbuch, part ii, vol. i.

self-sufficient, communities.   Consequently it was a period of particularism in thought.   Value was an object of reflection, not as a general conception, but only as applying to this or that good.   It was the worth of the thing in itself, not its power to procure other things in exchange that was thought of.   The value existed before an exchange was made, and as the common estimation of the community it was the criterion by which to justify the price.

At the close of the middle ages the two conditions came into existence as an effect partly of the growing activity in buying and selling, and the expansion of the circle of common economic interests, and partly of the replacement of local by national regulation which accompanied the breaking down of the feudal system and the development of the nation and state.   Not only was a "money economy" fully established, but industrial affairs were extensively discussed and written upon, and national policies were shaped largely by commercial interests.   Value became a general conception and was so commonly thought of as standing for the purchasing power of the good, that the term price, the concrete expression of that power, was used as a synonym.   But purchasing power was recognized as a characteristic of money before it was recognized as a characteristic of goods.   This is illustrated by Puffendorf's definition of "eminent price", and in the early mercantile theory that a nation in order to command purchasing power must possess money or treasure.   But with the enlargement of experience in trading, money gradually assumed the role of a mere instrument of exchange and goods were seen to be the beginning and the end of every transaction, to be the only final means of payment.   When the conception of exchange value was once grasped it became the predominant conception.   Locke announced exchange value to be the only kind of value of concern in economic discussions. He has been followed not only by the physiocrats, but by most modern economists until value in economics has generally come to mean exchange value.

We come now to the second feature of the evolution of the concept of value, namely, the recognition of value as subjective. Value is naturally thought of first objectively. Indeed, " value " is not thought of at all, but *the value*, which is conceived as a quality of the object valued. That value may be understood in the subjective sense it is necessary that it become an object of scientific thought. The question should be, not what ought to be the value, but what is value? The latter question was not asked until the former had occupied men's minds for a considerable period of time. Yet in those discussions which grew out of the desire to find rules for right conduct we find the foreshadowings of later subjective conceptions.

Aristotle saw that all economic activities are caused by the variable wants of mankind and considered demand to be the ultimate measure of value. But when he said that a just exchange is one by which equal value is given for equal value he obviously had objective value in mind. The schoolmen and canonists readily accepted this doctrine, but they never really understood the relation of demand to value. They recognized, however, the dependence of industry upon wants ; but they considered wants to be only the needs of man's physical nature. Those of his intellectual and emotional nature they called desires and considered them to belong to a different category. Utility was that quality by which goods satisfy wants and was carefully distinguished from the quality by which they satisfy desires, a mere pleasure-giving quality. Until these two conceptions could be reduced to one general idea, until a common element in both wants and desires could be perceived, and utility understood in a subjective sense, it was not possible to reach a conception of value as subjective. But the canonists made some advance in this direction when they admitted that the amount of value is affected by the strength of desires and included the pleasure-giving quality among the items to be considered in estimating the true value.

The dependence of value upon subjective utility, and hence the subjective nature of value, came to be more clearly recognized by later ecclesiastical writers, and it was prominent in the views of writers on natural law like Puffendorf. It was roughly perceived by Davanzati among empirical writers, and more clearly by Montanari, who devoted several pages to showing that wants in the sense intended by Aristotle included also desires. This position was taken by Nicholas Barbon, who held the satisfying of desires to be but the supplying of the wants of the mind. He recognized both value and utility to be subjective. Value, he maintained, depends upon the use of a thing for supplying wants which proceed mostly from the imagination. " The Mind changeth: the things grow out of use, and so lose their Value." [1]

These conceptions, occurring as they did in the discourses of but a few writers scattered over a long period, and by them set forth with great brevity, did not have much influence upon the common thought of the people. In this common thought, two kinds of value appeared : one an intrinsic quality of the thing, the other the quantity of it that can be had for a fixed quantity of another thing given in exchange for it. The latter was usually spoken of as price. Both these conceptions were objective. But John Locke who belonged in this line of thought, recognized that there could be

[1] *Ante* p. 59.

no such thing as an objective intrinsic value.   He
distinguished between the "intrinsic natural worth
of a thing," the later value-in-use, and the "marketable value" of any assigned quantity of the thing.
His conception of the latter was objective ; he described
the causes to which it is due as purely external, that is
as acting directly, not through the medium of the mind.
In this position we have seen he was closely followed by
Quesnay.   But the minds of the psychological writers,
Galiani, Turgot and Condillac were filled with the subjective idea of value, which in their writings reached full
and clear expression.

We have come now to the evolution of the conception
of the causes which determine the amount of value, the
evolution of the law of value.   The fundamental conception of the canonists was that the true or real value
of anything is the value of the labor ; that is, it is a fair
compensation for the toil of the producer.   The amount
of this compensation was thought to depend upon the
quality of the living customary in the class to which the
producer belonged.   It could be known only by the general opinion of the community.   The amount of a true
value was then a quantity ethically determined and rested
upon a judgment of what is fair to the producer.   The
canonists knew no law of value.   The common estimation by the community of what a thing is worth, was the
basis of the just price.   This, they thought, could not be
trusted to market conditions, but could only be ascertained by experts capable of interpreting this estimation.
But with the increase of commerce and the complication
of the economic system generally, the common estimation
came to be, and was understood to be, more and more
the product of elements quite different from the conception of a fair compensation ; such as changes in the goodness of the article, changes in the desires of the people,

special conditions as to want, and the state of supply. Its interpretation therefore, which needed to take into account all these items, became a matter of increasing difficulty. This just price itself, which was at first a single point, became a zone including a highest, a lowest, and a middle just price. As prices which were the results of competing forces would often fall within the limits of this zone, indeed would usually do so when the competition was equal, the canonists finally admitted, as appears by Scaccia, that under normal conditions the price of the market would be the just price.

But in the meantime changes were going on. The social system of place and service was giving way to one of contract and exchange. Nations were becoming conscious of their greatness, and commerce was looked upon as the instrument of national prosperity. The important question in regard to our subject was no longer, what constitutes the true value or the just price, but what decides the market price of goods, or the purchasing power of money? This was seen to be the action upon each other of two forces of which price is a result.

With Montanari these forces were the quantity of goods and the need of them, with Locke they were the quantity and the vent or effective demand. The important point is that the conception of value, from being the esteem in which a commodity ought to be held, an esteem the degree of which could be interpreted by experts only, had come to be its power in exchange. Hence, it is during this period rather than during that of the canonists, that the first indications of a law of value are to be found.

In the common thought of the period the old conception of the "true value" remained as intrinsic value, which was tacitly assumed to be equal to a proper recompense for costs. The real worth of anything was the trouble in cost to get it. Beyond this, cost of production is scarcely connected with value until the last half of the seventeenth century, when Petty and Locke bring it again into prominence. Their work was the beginning of a deeper analysis of the law of value.

During the next period the cultivation of the soil was held to be a better source of national prosperity than foreign commerce and thought turned from intermediate to ultimate causes of wealth. Those who were inclined to interpret the law of value mechanically held that while the temporary value in the market is the resultant of the counteraction of supply and demand, in the long run cost of production, by limiting both of these forces, is the permanent arbiter of value. They stated facts and relations, but gave little explanation of them. Their analysis of costs shows that they regarded causes as acting directly which could only act indirectly, and as simple and invariable which were in their nature most variable and complex. Thus needs and habits of the worker that determine his subsistence and the cost of production were to Cantillon and Quesnay simple, natural phenomena that could be easily estimated. The psychological writers, on the other hand, who attempted to describe the forces that oppose each other in determining value from internal causes found them to be complex and variable in a high degree. Their theory in brief was that these forces determine the personal valuations which are brought together in the market and compared, and that the market value and price is that upon which it is possible for the buyers and sellers to agree as a result of this comparison. Galiani and Condillac held the opposing forces in the primary contest to be utility and scarcity, Turgot, utility and cost.

That none of these earlier attempts to explain value are satisfactory is not to be wondered at when we consider the complexity of the phenomena, and when we remember that more than a century and a quarter has passed and there is yet no formulation of the law of value, that has met with general approval. But on the other hand so much was done that there is scarcely any proposition of importance in the modern discussion of value which was not either stated or suggested by the writers of this first period of economic science, and which had not been discussed before Adam Smith made political economy a world study.

LIST OF AUTHORITIES.

Aristotle, The Nicomachean ethics of. Translated by J. E. C. Welldon London, 1897.
—— The politics of. Translated by B. Jowett. Oxford, 1885.
Ashley, W. J. An introduction to English economic history and theory. New York and London, 1893.
Bevan, Wilson Lloyd. Sir William Petty ; a study in English economic literature. Pub. Amer. Econ. Ass'n, Vol. IX, No. 4.
Bonar, James. Philosophy and political economy. London, 1893.
Cantillon, R. Essai sur le commerce. Reprinted for Harvard University, Boston, 1892.
Cicero, M. Tullius. Orationes, In C. Verrem.
Cohn, Dr. Gustav. A history of political economy. Translated by Dr. Joseph Adna Hill. Ann. of Amer. Acad. sup., March, 1894.
Condillac, M. L'Abbé de. Le commerce et le gouvernment. Amsterdam, 1776.
Corpus Juris Civilis Justiniani. Institutiones et Digestum.
Cossa, Luigi. An introduction to the study of political economy. Translated by Louis Duer, M. A. London, 1893.
Cunningham, W. The growth of English industry and commerce. Cambridge : at the University Press, 1896.
Daire, Eugene M. Economistes financiers du XVIIIᵉ siècle, précédés de notices historiques sur chaque auteur, et accompagnés de commentaires et de notes explicatives. Paris, 1843.
Davanzati, Bernardo. Lezione della moneta. Scrittori classici Italiani di economia politica, Parte antica, tomo ii. Milano, 1804.
Dietzel, Heinrich. Theoretische Socialökonomik. Wagner's Lehrbuch, II, 1.
Dubois, A. Les theories psychologiques de la valeur au XVIIIᵉ siècle. Revue d'economic politique, 11 : 849.
Endemann, Dr. W. Studien in der Romanisch-kanonistischen Wirthschafts- und Rechtslehre. Berlin, 1874, 1883.
Erdmann, J. E. History of philosophy. English translation edited by W. S. Hough. London and New York, 1891.
Espinas, A. Histoire des doctrines economiques. Paris.
Galiani, Ferdinando. Della moneta. Scrittori classici Italiani di economia politica, Parte moderna, tomo iii, iv. Milano, 1804.
Graziani, Augusto. Storia critica della theoria del valore in Italia. Milano, 1889.
Goldschmidt, I. Handbuch des Handelsrechts, Universalgeschichte des Handelsrechts. vol. i. Stuttgart, 1891.

Grotius, Hugo. De jure belli et pacis. Accompanied by an abridged translation by William Whewell, D.D. Cambridge, 1853.

Grueber, Erwin. The Roman law of damage to property. Being a commentary on the title of the digest ad legem aquiliam (IX, 2). Oxford, 1886.

Higgs, Henry. The Physiocrats. Six lectures on the French economistes of the 18th century. London and New York, 1896.

Hull, Ch. H. The economic writings of Sir William Petty. Cambridge, 1899.

Hume, David. Essays, literary, moral and political. Reprint of the two vols., 8vo. ed. London, 1870.

Hutcheson, Francis. A system of moral philosophy. Glasgow, 1755.

Ingram, I. K. A history of political economy. With preface by Prof. E. J. James, Ph.D. New York, 1888.

Joubleau, M. Felix. Études sur Colbert. Paris, 1856.

Locke, John. Some considerations of the lowering of interest and raising the value of money. Works, vol. ii. London, 1726.

Locke, John. Two treatises of government. London, 1772.

McCulloch, J. R. The literature of political economy. London, 1865.

Mackintosh, James. The Roman law of sales. Digest XVIII, 1, and XIX, 1, translated. Edinburgh, 1892.

Montanari, Geminiano. Della moneta. Scrittori classici Italiani di economia politica, Parte antica, tomo iii. Milano, 1804.

Montchrétien, Antoyne de. Traicté de l'oeconomie politique dedié en 1615 au roy . . . avec introd. et notes par 7h. Funck-Brentano. Paris, 1889.

Moyle, J. B. The Institutes of Justinian translated into English. Oxford, 1889.

Mun, Thomas. England's treasure by forraign trade. 1664. Economic classics. New York and London. 1895.

Palgrave, Robert Henry Ingles. Dictionary of political economy. London, 1894–99.

Quesnay, F. Oeuvres économiques et philosophiques, publiées avec une introduction et des notes par A. Onken. Paris, 1888.

Plato, the dialogues of. Translated by B. Jowett. New York and London, 1892.

Puffendorf, Samuel. Law of nature and nations. Translated into English. Oxford, 1710.

Roscher, W. Geschichte der National Oekonomik in Deutschland. Munich, 1874.

Schelle, G. Du Pont de Nemours et l'école physiocratique. Paris, 1888.

Schmoller, Gustav. The mercantile system and its historical significance. Economic classics. New York, 1896.

Seneca, L. Annaeus. Opera quae supersunt. De beneficiis.

Smith, Adam. An inquiry into the nature and causes of the wealth of nations. London, 1786—4th edition.

—— Lectures delivered in the University of Glasgow in 1763. Edited by Edwin Cannan. Oxford, 1896.

Steuart, Sir James. An inquiry into the principles of political economy. London, 1767.

Stintzing, Roderick. Geschichte der populären Literatur des römisch-kanonischen Rechts in Deutschland. Leipzig, 1867.

Thomas Aquinas. Opera omnia, cum commentariis Thomae de Vio, Caietani. Antwerp, 1612.

Turgot. Oeuvres, nouvelle edition avec les notes de Dupont de Nemours, et précédée d'une notice sur la vie et les ouvrages de Turgot, par M. Eugene Daire. Paris, 1844.

—— Reflections on the formation and distribution of riches. 1770. Economic classics. New York, 1898.

Wagner, Adolph. Lehr und Handbuch der politischen Oekonomie, I, 1. Grundlagen der Volkswirthschaft. Leipzig, 1892.

Wiskemann, Heinrich. Darstellung der in Deutschland zur Zeit der Reformation herrschenden nationalökonomischen Ansichten. Leipzig, 1861.

Zuckerkandl, Dr. Robert. Zur Theorie des Preises mit besonderer Berücksichtigung der geschichtlichen Entwicklung der Lehre. Leipzig, 1889.

INDEX OF NAMES.